AWAKENING THE BELOW

AWAKENING THE BELOW
Navigating through Darkness and Spiritual Emergency

By
Oholomo

AEON

First published in 2025 by
Aeon Books

Copyright © 2025 by Oholomo

The right of Oholomo to be identified as the author of this work has been asserted in accordance with §§ 77 and 78 of the Copyright Design and Patents Act 1988.

All rights reserved. No part of this publication may be reproduced, stored in a retrieval system, or transmitted, in any form or by any means, electronic, mechanical, photocopying, recording, or otherwise, without the prior written permission of the publisher.

British Library Cataloguing in Publication Data

A C.I.P. for this book is available from the British Library

ISBN-13: 978-1-80152-198-7

Typeset by Medlar Publishing Solutions Pvt Ltd, India

www.aeonbooks.co.uk

CONTENTS

ACKNOWLEDGEMENTS   vii

WARNINGS AND CAVEATS   ix

CHAPTER ONE
The Buddha and the goddess   1

CHAPTER TWO
What is the Below?   7

CHAPTER THREE
Descent into the underworld   29

CHAPTER FOUR
Navigating the darkness   79

CHAPTER FIVE
Spiritual emergency or Descent into the Below? 127

CHAPTER SIX
Benediction 147

ACKNOWLEDGEMENTS

I want to sincerely thank the "Bottom-Up Awakening" discussion group that met with me over the course of about six months to provide feedback on portions of this book as I was writing them. I also want to thank the many friends who let me repeat or reproduce their stories here, including Jack, Misha, Jeff, Lisa, and Kini. Misha was particularly generous with her time, providing detailed feedback and copyediting on the entire book.

WARNINGS AND CAVEATS

Before you read any further, please read and take to heart the following warnings and caveats:

(1) I am not a medical professional or psychologist, and this book is intended as a work of art. Everything I am writing in this book is poetry not science, and definitely not an infallibly accurate prescription for you to follow. Please always listen to your own inner guidance when evaluating what is said here, and carefully determine if any of it is right for you. It's okay if it's not; just freely discard whatever doesn't work for you and go about your business with confidence that you know yourself best.

(2) These pages are intended to elicit a strong effect for certain readers. If you are not the intended reader, then it will all likely seem like complete gibberish to you. However, if you are in a Below-style awakening process, this book may be intensely psychoactive. It may take you on a profoundly personal and spiritual journey. If you are deep in the throes of the Below at this very moment, please be aware that reading these pages may have unexpected effects on you, including energy surges, deep emotions, insomnia, and other psychophysical effects. If you are prone to experiencing a lot of fear

in your awakening process, be aware that some of what I write here may well trigger that kind of response. Always take it in small doses, prioritizing your own well-being and safety.

(3) Don't ever let anything I say in this book talk you out of seeking assistance from a qualified therapist, counselor, or spiritual guide if you believe that kind of resource would be beneficial for you. Even though I am huge fan of DIY, I think that having someone, or a group of people, you check in with on a regular basis can be extremely helpful when you are navigating any awakening process. Just make sure you feel supported, cared for, and understood by them, and that your boundaries and autonomy are always respected. If you feel like something is off, you are most likely right.

(4) If you feel well resourced and mentally strong, then rest assured that the Descent into the Below is not a problem. Nothing is broken. There is nothing to change or fix. Always remember that this process is a blessing—a mysterious one that can be quite challenging at times, but a blessing all the same.

CHAPTER ONE

The Buddha and the goddess

Let's start with a story. It's a famous episode in the legendary life of the Buddha that you probably already know. In the tale, the future Buddha, Siddhartha Gotama, had left behind his wife and child, his position as the crown prince of his kingdom, and his life of luxury and ease in order to take up the path of a forest recluse. For years as a samanera (i.e., a person who has renounced worldly life to become a spiritual seeker), he had given himself over to the practice of austere asceticism, intense meditation, and other yogic practices that the gurus of his day promised would lead to enlightenment. In the process, he had starved himself, deprived himself of sleep, performed all kinds of physically painful self-deprivations, and denied himself every biological and psychological comfort in a single-minded pursuit of this lofty goal.

After many years of this kind of practice, having become adept at many states of consciousness but also having become exhausted and on the verge of starvation, he finally had determined that this path was too extreme. He therefore had acquiesced to his bodily needs and had eaten his first decent meal in a long time. Having arranged himself a seat under a bodhi tree, he had then set off on a different tack. Having remembered a certain experience of peaceful focus he had as a child, he had decided to recall that state and use it as a platform from which to achieve nirvana. He had taken a strong determination then and there that he would not arise from the foot of the tree until he became awakened. Give me enlightenment or give me death! The hero's strength, resolve, and determination (they say "he was a lion among men") are a large part of what has allowed this legend to speak to generations of followers over the past two and a half millennia.

But now, as he approaches the point of victory in his quest, the samanera faces his ultimate challenge. In the climax of the myth's story-arc, he is accosted by a horde of evil spirits led by Mara, the demon king. Some retellings of this narrative take up a great deal of text describing the fearsome attributes of these demons and their malicious threats toward Siddhartha. In certain versions, Mara's three daughters (representing desire, aversion, and attachment) try to knock him off his seat by tempting him with their sensual wiles. Through it all, the samanera is invariably depicted as aloof and equanimous, completely unfazed by any attack or temptation.

For centuries, Buddhist commentators have interpreted an encounter with Mara—whether in this myth of the Buddha or in other scriptures—both literally and figuratively. Literalists see demonic forces opposing serious meditators as external entities lying in wait to trip them up and derail their spiritual progress. Others have preferred to view these "demons" as internal psychological forces: the temptations, delusions, traumas, existential fears, and self-doubts that naturally arise as one progresses on the spiritual path. From this perspective, Mara himself represents the last thrashes of the separate ego-self grasping for any point of stability as it nears the point of being defeated once and for all. Although the encounter with Mara may be understood in these different ways, ultimately everyone agrees that anyone on a quest to awaken sooner or later must encounter their own horde of demons.

In the version of the Buddha's myth told by the eighteenth-century Tibetan Tenzin Chögyel (translated for Penguin Classics by Kurtis R. Schaeffer), Mara's assault takes up all of chapter nine. The demonic horde rains weapons down upon the resolute meditator, but the samanera's compassion turns them all into flowers. Enraged by Siddhartha's equipoise, the demon king challenges Siddhartha's worthiness to become enlightened. On what basis does he take that seat under the bodhi tree? How dare Siddhartha think that he has earned that right?

Siddhartha (here referred to as "the Bodhisattva") calmly responds to these taunts by placing his hand upon the ground, and calling the earth to bear witness to the fact that he has made "endless sacrifices" in lifetime after lifetime of practicing virtue. Just then,

> the ground trembled, and Sthavara, goddess of the earth, emerged halfway out of the soil. She folded her hands in reverence to the Bodhisattva. "Great One, it is so," she said. "It is just as you have declared. The truth of this is evident to me. And yet, Lord, now you have become the witness for the world and the gods."

With these words, Mara is defeated. After mounting a few last attempts to scare Siddhartha in vain, he finally retreats. Now in the clear, the samanera settles into a deep meditative state and concludes his quest to transcend the human condition. He realizes the so-called Four Noble Truths: that life is suffering; that the cause of suffering is desire, aversion, and ignorance; that these can be eliminated; and that the path to their elimination involves virtue, meditation, and insight into the true nature of consciousness. This discovery earns him the title "Buddha," meaning "Awakened One." Other names he would come to be known by include "the Victorious One," "the Transcendent One," "the Unsurpassed," and other epithets that connote his victorious struggle of rising above the forces of evil and ignorance.

This story I have just told has inspired countless generations of seekers, and continues to do so today. It is a perfectly tailored description of a model of spirituality that in this book I will call "Awakening the Above." While there are other examples from world mythology, the Buddha is the paramount example of this transcendent trajectory. Awakening the Above means to wake up from the delusions and suffering of the ordinary world, to escape from the limitations of the human body and mind, and to be victorious over the ego, psychological turmoil, and other forces of Darkness. All of the details in the Buddha's story line are pointing toward the Above: he leaves his family and his society behind, transcends his biological body and his mind, controls his emotions, defeats the demons, and is the paragon of determination and virtue. He masters all methods of meditation and makes "endless sacrifices" to deserve his awakening. Such is the momentum behind his trajectory of transcendence that no one can stand in his way—even the earth goddess herself bows down and cedes her place of honor to him.

But what if the legend of the Buddha's life were to be written from a different perspective? What if it were written as a myth about "Awakening the Below"? How would the story be told differently?

Well, for one thing, that climactic moment in the narrative where Siddhartha lays his hand upon the earth would need to be heavily revised. Imagine if, rather than rising up out of the earth to bear witness to his virtue, the goddess were instead to pull the demon-besieged Siddhartha down into the earth, and press his emaciated, battered body against her warm breast. Imagine if, while she held him, the demon horde fully engulfed him, like a dark cloud permeating his every cell. Imagine if all of his past traumas, his deepest fears, his memories, his longings, his tears, his rage, and his broken-heartedness were through this act of love alchemized into an infinite field of unspeakable tenderness. Imagine if instead of being the dispassionate witness of the world, he instead merged with the world's soul in all of its woundedness and interconnection. Imagine if, instead of vanquishing the demons, he accepted and welcomed them as parts of himself.

What do you think? Can you visualize a world like this, where Awakened Ones don't have to be brave heroes? Where there is as much space for vulnerability and helplessness as there is for virtue and resolve? Where tropes of masculine power and victory make way for the gentle, loving intimacy of the divine feminine? Where it is not by vanquishing suffering that Siddhartha becomes enlightened, but by surrendering to it? Where instead of transcending his humanity, he deeply inhabits and embodies it in all of its fragility, vulnerability, and tenderness? Where instead of defeating Mara, he discovers that the Dark is as sacred as the Light?

How does our version of the story end if there's no need for the hero to become the "World-honored One"? Perhaps the Buddha will open his eyes only to realize that it was all just a dream and he is back in bed in the palace. Maybe he puts his arm around his sleeping wife, the beautiful young Yasodhara, and lovingly kisses her naked shoulder as he falls back to sleep. Maybe he realizes he doesn't need to be the victor after all, perhaps wishing for nothing more than to return to his ordinary life in service to his family and his people.

However the ending of this new myth might be written, the essence of the story will emphasize that awakening the Below is less about transcendence or perfection than it is about intimacy. It's less about waking *up from* life than it is about waking *down into* it, gathering up all of the fractured dimensions of our being and weaving the broken pieces into a scarred yet sacred wholeness.

Before you get the wrong idea about what I'm saying here, let me be clear: this book is not arguing that one of these two versions of the Buddha myth is better than the other. It is not about pitting Above against Below, producing a dualism to take sides over. Rather, my basic premise in these pages is simply to establish that descent into the Below is a viable, legitimate—but quite different—path of spiritual development than we get from stories about spiritual heroes and demon-vanquishers. This book is about making space for the Below alongside more Above-oriented approaches from Buddhism, Advaita Vedanta, and other popular spiritual approaches.

From what I have seen, it seems that some people are naturally oriented toward the Below, and that they will spontaneously discover themselves moving in that direction (or will be thrust into it kicking and screaming!) when they begin to undergo an awakening process. Without any background knowledge to help contextualize what is going on, surprise openings to the Below can be difficult to understand. They are consequently often interpreted as "spiritual emergencies" or mental health crises rather than the blessings and opportunities that they truly can be. My motivation in writing this book is to validate and normalize such experiences, in order to encourage people to embrace and even lean into the precious dark wisdom that comes from Below.

Finally, this book is also an invitation for those who find themselves naturally drawn toward Above-based spirituality to become more aware of the Below, to become less fearful or dismissive of it, and potentially even to open up to exploring some of this territory. While our natural inclinations may draw us Above or Below, the other is always available for us to investigate, if we are so called. Ultimately, as we will discuss, these two paths converge, becoming inseparable or even indistinguishable. As far as this book is concerned, the true goal of spirituality is nothing short of this unity of Above and Below, the integration of both into a seamless whole.

CHAPTER TWO

What is the Below?

In this book I am using "Above" and "Below" as metaphors referring to whole clusters of experiences, ideas, practices, symbols, and realizations that can arise in the course of an awakening process. These metaphors should not be taken as literal or precise descriptions. If there's one thing that every single tradition has agreed upon, it's that words cannot possibly be adequate to capture the ineffably mystical nature of spiritual experiences. Let's agree to use these metaphorical phrases as pointers to a range of experiences, without confusing the finger with the moon.

My choice of using the specific metaphors Above and Below is deliberate. When I first began speaking about this topic, I initially was drawn to using the words Spirit and Soul. However, I soon found out that this distinction had already been popularized among depth psychologists and in certain spiritual communities by the prominent Jungian theorist John Hillman. I therefore wanted to use terminology that had fewer preconceived clinical notions packaged into them, and felt that Above and Below would be more neutral. I am aware that there is a similar usage of the terms "Awakening from Above" and "Awakening from Below" in some Jewish traditions, but this is not where I got the terms from and these are not common terms in mainstream Western spirituality, so I don't mean to invoke any of those specific connotations.

Even so, there are undeniable similarities between my model and these ways of speaking, as well as with other approaches that identify two types or orientations of spirituality. Friedrich Nietzsche, for example, influentially distinguished between the Apollonian and Dionysian impulses he identified in Ancient Greek culture, based on differences between the mythologies and rituals associated with these two deities. In his model, the god Apollo was associated with the sun, rationality, heroism, and order, while Dionysius was associated with intoxication, ecstasy, emotion, and chaos. At first glance, these are not entirely dissimilar from what I am going for with the terms Above and Below.

More recently, an analogous split has been identified in ancient India by the scholar of religion David Gordon White, who in books such as *Kiss of the Yogini* distinguishes between the Dharma-based current in Indian religion versus the various Tantric goddess traditions. The former (characterized mainly by male deities) tended to value order, morality, wisdom, and meditative practices focused on stillness, while the latter (centering the feminine) tended to involve ecstatic trances, intoxication, ritual sex, and sensual pleasure. Again, at first glance, a lot of that fits with my model of Above and Below.

Other models that overlap substantially with what I have written here include Mircea Eliade's and Michael Harner's notions of shamanism, which strongly distinguish between the overworld and the underworld, as well as Carl G. Jung's notion of the ego's descent into the wilds of the shadows of the psyche. While I learned about all of these models through reading scholarly books on them, this book you are holding in your hands is emphatically not an academic one. It is a personal one. So, when I use the terms Above and Below here in these pages, I am not intending to make historical or theoretical distinctions. What concerns us here is not the accuracy of these categories for describing particular cultural, religious, or spiritual traditions, but rather their emotional and poetic valence in describing the qualities of our own individual spiritual experiences. I am trying to paint an intuitive, subjective, and emotional picture, not a literal one.

As Above, so Below

I am going to spend a bit of time in this chapter trying to define more precisely what I am talking about when I say "the Below." Let me start with Figure 1, where I offer a map of the simplest version of the model I am proposing.

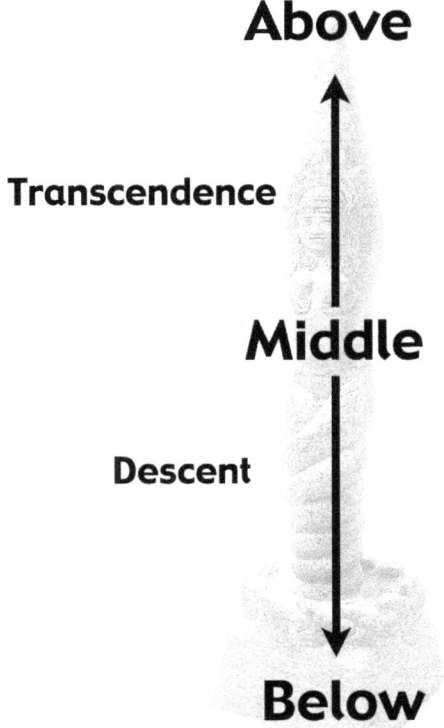

Figure 1. The three realms and two trajectories.

In the center of this image lies the Middle, the realm where we humans ordinarily spend the majority of our lives. In this domain, I experience myself as an ego (what many people call the separate self or the narrative self) with a material body. It is from this perspective that non-awakened people typically experience pretty much all of their everyday activities, relationships, and identities related to work, family, hobbies, and so forth.

The quest for fulfillment in the Middle realm involves developing one's personality, intellectual interests, creative outlets, and social connections. We use these skills to become adept at whatever challenges, missions, or tasks our society and culture set out for us. In the modern West, some milestone achievements of the Middle include becoming established in a career, achieving financial independence, finding a mate, raising a family, and finding a meaningful way to contribute to solving some of our most pressing social problems. Personal healing and growth in the Middle are often facilitated by interactions with therapists, coaches, teachers, parents, and other mentors, who help us to work on our physical, psychological, and social well-being. We don't usually refer to these pursuits as spiritual, but I would argue that, ultimately, integrating spiritual realizations back into our Middle lives is precisely the point of spirituality. More on that later.

In any case, not all people are moved in this lifetime to explore the territory beyond the Middle. For that reason, mainstream spiritual and religious opportunities tend to stay within its boundaries. Religious institutions operating in this domain teach morality and kindness, and promise a comfortable afterlife. Spiritual teachers and communities operating at this level include mainstream yoga and mindfulness classes focused on well-being, and teachings about praying or manifesting your way into wealth and happiness. Shamanism and magick that ultimately are serving egoic, psychological, or material ends are also examples of Middle-based practices, although they might claim to be otherwise. These forms of spirituality frequently offer beneficial practices, but the benefits they hold out are limited to the ordinary, everyday human world.

When one's quest for meaningful answers begins to look beyond the bounds of the ordinary and everyday, there are essentially two paths to choose from. Actually, people rarely make a conscious choice between them; more likely they are intuitively drawn in one direction or the other—or for some people, toward both simultaneously.

Those individuals drawn toward the Above are enticed by the promise of transcending the human condition, elevating oneself above suffering and "worldly" concerns and discovering the "ultimate truth" about the universe. Escaping the bondage of the ego and the physical form through a journey into the Above is what I call Transcendence. Traditions that emphasize this trajectory include Theravada Buddhism, Advaita Vedanta, and Christian mysticism, all traditions that have had a huge impact on Western spirituality.

What does the final goal of liberation look like in Above-based traditions? From Theravada we get the ideal of the serene monk, living in perpetual meditative bliss. Advaita has a similar idealized view of the Hindu sage (Ramana Maharshi comes to mind). Christianity likewise has its monks and nuns who ideally live lives of chastity and faith while preaching love and virtue (think of St. Francis of Assisi, for example). Traditions that prioritize this Transcendent trajectory consider the ultimate goal of spiritual practice to be to see through and rise above the vicissitudes of samsara (the everyday life of the Middle) once and for all, and then to reside permanently in the tranquility and bliss of Transcendence.

As they begin to open up to the Above through various spiritual practices, practitioners may experience a range of phenomena that pertains to this realm. In the most general terms, the first-person experience of "awakening the Above" involves four main aspects. First, and most characteristically, there is a shift in identity that transcends the personal, separate ego-self of the Middle. In Advaita and other Hindu-influenced systems, this is normally talked about as a shift in identification from the ego-self to the True Self, Pure Consciousness, or Brahman. In Christian mystical systems, the shift is from identification with the ego-self to identification as God, Christ, Child of God, Bride of Christ, or other terms. Buddhist systems speak of the dropping away of identification altogether, which they normally refer to as Non-self or Emptiness. In all cases, the ego-self is seen as less and less relevant as the trajectory of Transcendence continues, ultimately disappearing altogether from the practitioner's experience.

A second, equally important, aspect of the Above is the dissolution of perception. Generally, this involves the breaking down of the mental constructs that interpret the world as being composed of discrete physical objects, as well as seeing into the constructed nature of sensory perception. Again, there's a difference between how traditions express this. Hindu systems will tend to speak of this as the realization that all phenomena are "made out of consciousness" or are "inseparable from Brahman" or "part of the Self." Christianity will refer to this as the realization that all phenomena are "part of God" or "have a Divine nature." Buddhists, as always preferring the language of negation, tend to emphasize the Emptiness, non-arising, non-existence, or mirage-like nature of all phenomena.

Both of these aspects of the Above, the shift in identity and the dissolution of perception, are referred to in contemporary Western spiritual circles as nonduality. Some systems of Above-based spirituality, such as the teachings normally referred to as "radical nonduality," hold these realizations to be the only goal of spirituality. However, most traditional forms of Above-based spirituality teach one to discover and to interweave these strands of nonduality with other aspects or dimensions of the Above. One of the most common is a sense of sacredness—either experienced as gods, goddesses, or angelic beings, or else in shapeless, nebulous, or formless manifestations such as radiant light, bliss, joy, peace, and so forth. It is not unusual as part of awakening the Above to experience oneself fully merging with this sacredness or becoming divine. Experiences like this bring healing, wisdom, blessings, and other positive sensations. Eventually, it can settle down into a pervasive but gentle sweetness or tenderness that is a common background feature of all reality.

Another aspect that is often present in Above-based teachings is the opening of the heart. An open heart overflows with kindness and good will. Again, it is spoken about differently by different traditions, but think of the Buddhist practice of loving kindness meditation, the activities of Ama the Hindu hugging saint, or the symbol of the Virgin Mary or the sacred heart of Jesus. The shared idea here is a universal love that is extended globally regardless of the specific details or circumstances. Another feature of an open heart is that it can be easily heartbroken, filled with empathy, or even feel like it is taking on the suffering of the world. These two varieties of love—kindness and sensitivity—are the two sides of the same open-hearted coin.

While these four aspects are core experiential features of the Above, there are many other experiences that are reported and prized by different traditions. These include things like communication with disembodied teachers, psychic phenomena of various kinds, energetic flows, bodily bliss, auras, lights, colors, synchronicities, psychokinesis, and much more. There are a lot of books out there on all of this, so I'm not going to go into any more detail about any of it here. Let's just suffice it to say that all of this Above stuff differs markedly from the Below.

I am going to discuss the experiences of the Below in much more detail in coming chapters. For now, let's simply give a list of terms that can convey a general sense of the territory: bodily intelligence, sexual energy, emotions, trauma, the earth, the elements, ancestors, spirits, ghosts, demons, the imaginal, the soul, the dark feminine. Rather than Transcending up and beyond our individual humanity, in the Below we Descend, sinking down into and inhabiting the deepest layers of our embodiment and our psyche. Parallels to this Descent are perhaps suggested in Greek mythology in the form of the *katabasis*, or the descent into the underworld. A clear Below-oriented model is found in Jungian-influenced systems of depth psychology focused on the exploration of the darkness and liminality of the unconscious. Shamanism gives us another example, where the classic Descent trajectory involves a "shamanic crisis": an illness or existential event that brings the journeyer to the brink of death, which occasions an encounter with the deepest dimension of the soul.

In my experience, the majority of spiritual seekers who talk about "awakening" in the contemporary West are exclusively thinking about the Above, and may be completely unaware of the Below, or even hold negative views about it. These biases are not their fault. The narrative about the Buddha defeating Mara, discussed in the preface, is an influential myth that strongly shapes people's ideas of what "proper" spirituality looks like. Christianity's millennia-long tradition of characterizing the Below as Satanic and sinful also plants seeds of fear, distrust, and disdain in Western spiritual seekers (even those who eschew Christianity). Buddhism, Christianity, and Advaita all denigrate sexuality and sensual pleasure, whether as a form of greed and self-gratification or as an immoral act that is offensive to God. This can often set up a guilt-and-shame dynamic between Above-oriented spiritual seekers and many experiences in the Below.

As a consequence of prejudices such as these, many Western people who are experiencing an awakening process know nothing about the Below or even actively demonize it. However, in talking with people over the past years, I have noticed that a certain percentage of these people may nonetheless find themselves spontaneously thrust into the Below in the course of an awakening process. When this happens, it is common for spiritual journeyers to be thoroughly confused about why their awakenings don't seem to match those of their colleagues or fit into the maps they have been given. They may realize that they're on a different track than the norm, but have taken to understanding the Above as the "right" kind of awakening and the Below as a deviant or harmful cul-de-sac. Many people I have spoken to have come to believe that there's something wrong with them personally; that they are deficient or broken in some way that is hindering or preventing their spiritual growth. I also know people who have had more extreme reactions to the Below, such as believing that they have gone mad, checking themselves into mental hospitals, and going on psychiatric medication to stop what they assume must be symptoms of psychosis or other mental illnesses.

The purpose of this book is to help people recognize the signs of the Below when they appear, to navigate this territory more confidently, and to fully integrate these experiences into their spiritual development in a healthy and meaningful way. Helping journeyers to better understand and benefit from the Below begins by doing away with the prejudices and hierarchies we have inherited from various traditional sources. While the founders and followers of the world's religious and spiritual traditions may have expressed strong opinions about which kinds of experiences are better than others, we can and should do our own investigations and come to our own conclusions. In this book, I will share my own ideas based on my own personal explorations. My basic premise is that the Above and Below each hold out unique opportunities for growth, fulfillment, wisdom, and liberation. Those of us who find ourselves in the Below—whether by choice or by chance—can feel confident in the knowledge that it is a great blessing.

The idea that there are blessings in the Below may seem counterintuitive to you if you have been used to dismissing or denigrating this realm, or if you are experiencing a lot of fear about it. But I am far from the first person to have made this discovery. Many years ago, the comparative mythologist Joseph Campbell popularized the phrase "Return with Elixir," which I like quite a bit. He was referring to the final stage in what he called the "Hero's Journey," the narrative arc of many a mythological narrative, literary work, and even Hollywood movie. This is the point in the journey where the protagonist, having faced the darkness and threat of annihilation and having come out the other side, now returns back to the everyday world with a valuable boon (the elixir) for their community. For an example of this pattern, think of the seer who traveled through the ghost world and is now back in the village serving as a healer and counselor to her people. Or the myth of Jesus being crucified, only to then rise from the dead to guide his followers to salvation.

In the last decade or so, I have noticed that Western spirituality is increasingly placing importance on a particular Above-based variation of Return with Elixir, which these days is commonly referred to as Embodiment. If Transcendence is "waking up" (notice the

Above-oriented language), then Embodiment is often called "waking down," bringing one's awakening down into the physical body and into the material world. Instead of the recluse who leaves society in order to live in a state of permanent bliss, the ideal here is the bodhisattva, an awakened being who lives in the world compassionately integrating their enlightenment back into everyday life. In Zen Buddhism this is commonly referred to as "returning to the marketplace with gift-bestowing hands," after a famous series of paintings and poems called the Ten Oxherding Pictures. Tantric Buddhism (aka Vajrayana), Kashmiri Shaivism, and Daoist traditions each teach a whole suite of physical, breath, energy, visualization, deity, and meditative practices designed to integrate awakening into the body. Christianity, of course, has its own take on Embodiment, whereby God himself descends in the human form of Jesus in order to spread his love in the world of suffering and sin. What these traditions all share is the notion that residing eternally in the Above is not enough; one has to bring the elixir back down to the Middle.

The traditional myth of the Buddha's enlightenment I told in the preface also has a Return with Elixir. In the original telling, the Buddha defeats Mara by exhibiting a detached posture of equanimity, an appreciation of impermanence, and resolve in the face of suffering. This allows him to bring back the elixirs of Dharma—that is, teachings on how to transcend the human condition—from the Above. However, in my modified retelling, the Buddha would bring back altogether different elixirs from the Below. What are those gifts and how do we access them? That's what this book is about.

An example of awakening the Below

When I say "awakening the Below," I am not just referring to brief glimpses of the Below, but an awakening process that involves extended journeys into the Below or that, at least for a time, feels like the center of gravity is located in the Below. Here, I am going to give you just a taste of what awakening the Below can look like by briefly outlining my own story. (Keep in mind that this is just one example and that details can vary significantly.)

My spiritual explorations began when I was in elementary school. By the time I graduated from college, I had learned two forms of East Asian martial arts, served for several years as assistant to a sweat lodge ceremonialist, taken courses on shamanism and Asian religion, danced publicly with my power animals, experimented with earth magick, and taken psychedelics a few times. I had also read classical Buddhist, Hindu, and Daoist scriptures, and had become curious about yoga and meditation. I did not know enough at that time to differentiate between Above and Below, but in retrospect I clearly felt drawn in both directions.

After graduation, I lived in Asia for several years, continuing to vacillate between Above and Below. I spent many months at Buddhist meditation centers, monastic retreats, and long-term retreats at yoga ashrams. I became an energy healing practitioner. And I learned how to ritually honor nature spirits and other unseen beings from various kinds of "spirit doctors." During this time, I began to viscerally feel the difference between Above and Below, and I felt acutely torn between these two seemingly incompatible directions of growth and development.

It was during this time, when I was staying at a Buddhist monastery, that I had my first major spiritual breakthrough, a heart-opening experience that blew me open with universal compassion. After that heart opening, things were relatively stable for nearly twenty years while I established myself in my career and raised two children. However, in my mid-forties, I had another dramatic spiritual opening, this time a classic nondual awakening experience. This experience came on as I was listening to a ten- or fifteen-minute description of a technique called Headless Way. (I find it highly ironic that I had listened to countless in-depth descriptions of Buddhist and Hindu contemplative techniques for decades without any dramatic results, but a quirky British guy gushing about how he can't find his head somehow broke through!)

Anyway, you can read more about the details of my whole awakening process on my website, AwakeningTheBelow.com. Here, I just want to give the basic outline. As it happened, this initial glimpse of "headlessness" set off a series of dramatic mystical experiences over the next four years. Initially, these had to do with deepening into nonduality. My identity shifted from the ego-self to awareness, and six months later from awareness to non-self. I experienced rushes of Kundalini energy up my spine and out the top of my crown. My sensory perception started to dissolve as I began to experience the emptiness of all phenomena, and I had a few "cessation events" where consciousness turned off.

If you're following along, you'll have noticed that, so far, while I had a certain earlier proclivity for the Below, the truly impactful spiritual openings I had in my life were all oriented toward the Above. I could easily find analogues for everything I was experiencing in the Buddhist and Hindu teachings I knew well, and I could easily share them with others within my spiritual circles and be readily understood. Things felt amazing and I was certain I was on a trajectory to becoming enlightened.

All of that remained true for the first year or so after the awakening process began. However, after that point, my trajectory took a downward turn, into the Below, and things started getting much weirder. Over the following two years, I continued to have Above-style experiences that made sense to me based on my background in Asian traditions, but I simultaneously began to experience a whole range of Below-style phenomena. These began when the flow of Kundalini energy in my spine reversed direction, strongly gushing downward from my crown into the depths of my pelvis. I felt like something had been deposited in my hara, a dark gemstone that now seemed to take over and became the "engine" behind my awakening process. After that, I started to feel that my body was an autonomous intelligence with its own kind of embodied consciousness and sensitivity, and that it was teaching me how to sink more deeply into its depths of emotion and trauma.

My whole subtle body system lit up with each chakra being clearly defined and vibrantly alive with an energy that was at once blissful, sensual, and erotic. During this time, I was visited frequently by nature spirits, elementals, ancestors, goddesses, angels, and other ethereal beings that taught me valuable lessons and played a hand in orchestrating my spiritual journey. I navigated encounters with a few intensely dark denizens of the spirit world, and had a near brush with madness and death. Two years into the process, deep in the depths of the Below, I encountered a bottomless abyss of fear, and on the other side of it, the radiant divine light of my soul.

One thing worth mentioning about this period is that, although I had been steeped in Asian spiritual ideas and practices, the experiences I had in the Below felt much more closely aligned with my family heritage, which is predominantly Latin American, with both European and Indigenous roots. For example, the spirits that were the most significant guides on my journey all turned out to be Catholic figures, Pagan deities, or animals and plants native to South America rather than Buddhas or bodhisattvas. Another notable facet of my own process (as a cisgendered heterosexual male) was the predominance of feminine forms. Most of my most important spirit guides were female. My energy body felt like it had transformed into a feminine form. When I saw my soul, the form it took was that of a goddess.

These qualities of my experiences perplexed me. They seemed to be so far off the map of the familiar Asian traditions that, for a while, I was not sure if I was having an awakening experience or if I was going insane. Fortunately, I was well-resourced enough to be able to keep my wits about me while I gradually made some sense of what was happening. My earlier exposure to Indigenous traditions, shamanism, spirit healing, and energy work, along with nearly twenty-five years of daily yoga practice and deep study of religion, had all prepared me for exactly this kind of work.

After several months struggling to understand and trust the process, I decided to surrender to it. The message was coming loud and clear from my guides that I needed to integrate Above and Below into a coherent whole, and I took this to heart. I consulted books by authors who were adept at navigating these kinds of experiences, and created my own synthesis of practices that resonated with my unique experiences. Over the course of the next three years, I created an amalgamation of energetic, ancestral, shamanic, magickal, sexual, yogic, heart-opening, devotional, visualization, and meditation practices. I will describe the ingredients in that synthesis in Chapter Four. (Of course, the whole idea here is to encourage you to create your own DIY tools, so I am just giving you some starting points for your consideration.)

There will be a lot more to say in the coming pages about how certain practices can help you to open up to the Below and to unlock the blessings and gifts that it offers. However, if you would permit me to share the single most significant insight I learned from my own journey with you right now, I would say that it was the importance of surrender. This is going to be the major overarching theme in this book. To sum up my whole message in the most pithy form, it is that if you fully surrender to the Below, it will reveal its blessings.

Completing the circuits

This book is for those who find themselves on a similar path to mine. We have been to the Above; we have seen clearly the nondual, empty, divine nature of reality. Yet now, for who knows what reasons, we find that the techniques we mastered in the Above don't seem to be working for us anymore. We are intuitively feeling that we are being called to something deeper, more feminine, more intimate, more human, more alive.

If you have already begun to awaken the Below, you may have been feeling lost, or even trapped, down here. Perhaps you have felt scared and lonely, thinking that things have gone wrong or that you've gone crazy. If that's true, I am here to tell you that awakening the Below is a great blessing. You may not be able to see this yet, but your journey into the Below and the elixirs you will learn to bring back are absolutely critical to the evolution of your community and to humanity as a whole. We need you to be doing the work you are doing—in fact, the entire cosmos is depending on it. Thank you, most deeply, for every step you're taking on this journey!

Perhaps, for some readers, despite the difficulties you might be facing, you may already have begun to suspect that great blessings lie in the Below. Have you perhaps felt like purely Above-based awakenings are missing something? I mean, thank goodness that we have people who have gone far, far out into the Above and brought back those teachings. They are like beacons of light for the rest of us, and I am super grateful to them for doing that! But, aren't you a bit bored with enlightenment that lacks an equal amount of soulfulness? Awakened people who can't deeply inhabit their bodies, cook food with friends, or love their children madly? Awakened people who can't feel deep in their bones their own woundedness, the intergenerational trauma of racism, or the brutalization of the planet? Awakened people who can't light a candle for their ancestors, cry over the evening news, get lost in a piece of music, or have wild sex in the back seat of their car? I know I have.

Figure 2 adds to our simple model the culmination of both trajectories I've been talking about. What this book is calling for is the completion of both circuits: fully awakened beings who are also fully human. Awakenings that both Transcend to the farthest reaches of the Above and Descend to the farthest reaches of the Below, and then Embody and Return to integrate all of the gifts, wisdom, perspectives, and other elixirs gathered along the way back into the everyday for the benefit of all of life.

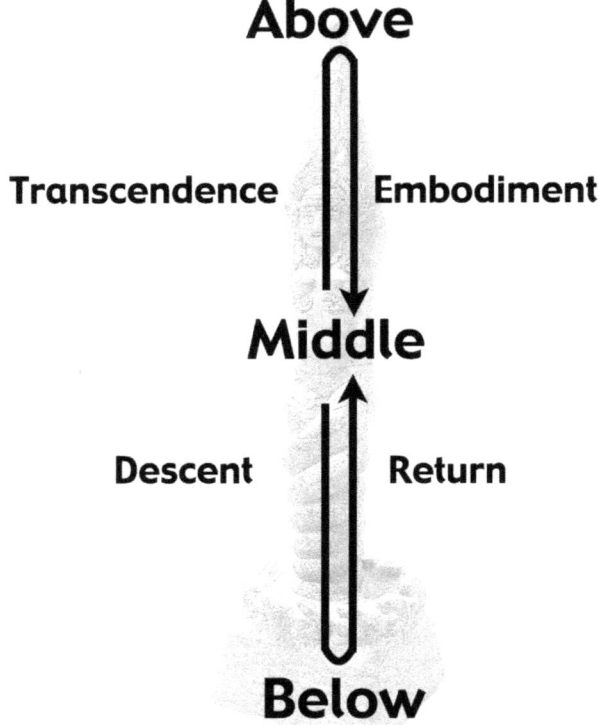

Figure 2. Completing the journeys.

What does completion look like? Eventually, once you have traversed both of the loops shown in Figure 2, you will discover that you are able to shift your consciousness back and forth at will between the Above, the Below, and the Middle. (Of course, the Middle will have transformed for you; it will still be the domain of the personality and the everyday, but now it is no longer dominated by the ego or the idea that the body is merely physical.) Different people may experience this flexibility in different ways. For me, I could draw my energy into different regions of my body, which caused my consciousness to sink or rise into these three realms. But, again, that's me; your experience will likely vary.

However it happens for you, once you can freely shift your consciousness in that way, the elixirs of the three realms will start flowing together. You will then gradually experience the Above, Below, and Middle begin to cohere. From the Above, you will have learned definitively and permanently the nondual nature of reality. You will find yourself expressing an open heart that is unambiguously compassionate toward all beings. You will recognize and fully embody your own radiant divine nature. From the Below, you will have gathered a deep intimacy with the living intelligence of your human body as well as with the natural environment. You will have reconciled ancestral, intergenerational, and past life traumas. You will have received the blessing and protection of spirit guides, angels, and deities. You will have worked through your deepest fears to discover and become totally aligned with your soul's mandate.

Bringing everything I've just said back into the Middle, you will achieve well-being and balance as an individual operating in the ordinary world, whatever that looks like for you. You will have inhabited (not erased!) your old wounds so thoroughly that you will overflow with presence and empathy in all of your relationships. You will become an effective channel to deliver your deepest gifts to your society and culture. And you will manifest your unique blend of elixirs in everything you do in your daily activities of work, family, and community. Your work of living out your awakening in the world will not be finished—in fact, it never will be—but the three realms will forevermore be integrated, whole, and inseparable parts of one seamless awakened singularity.

This kind of awakening is something that unfolds over the long term—years or even decades. So, if you feel trapped in the Below right now, try not to worry too much. It's just a sign that you haven't gotten to the bottom quite yet. Eventually, though, when you have passed through the final trial (which I call the Abyss; see Chapter Three), your Return will naturally and effortlessly begin without your needing to do anything. Likewise, if you haven't yet completed the Transcendence portion of your journey, don't worry about that either. That can be completed before, during, or after your transit through the Below, and it will happen just as effortlessly. (In my case, which isn't to be thought of as the norm, I started the Transcendence first, then did the Embodiment and Descent roughly simultaneously, and then completed the Return.) Wherever you are in your own trajectory, just surrender to being right there. You will discover that there are elixirs to be found absolutely everywhere.

Useful resources

Before we jump into the remainder of the book, I wanted to briefly mention a few other explorations of the Below that I have personally found interesting and inspirational. I also will make explicit how these models are different than mine.

First and foremost of these, in my opinion, is the model forwarded by Bill Plotkin in his book *The Journey of Soul Initiation* (2021). I will admit that the impact this book had on me was like no other I can remember in a very long time. I found it after I had completed my own journey into the depths of the Below, and after I had already formulated in my own language a lot of the ideas that are now being given expression in this book. However, in reading Plotkin's work, I immediately recognized a fellow explorer of the same territory. (Actually, in the book, he traces the trajectories of a half dozen or so people as they traversed the Below, so I recognized *multiple* fellow explorers.) It's a brilliant book, which I highly recommend.

There are many similarities between Plotkin's book and the one you are holding in your hands right now. Some are due to the influence that Plotkin has had on me, such as the fact that I was inspired by Plotkin's use of stories, and have emulated that approach here. A substantial amount of the similarity is because we are both tremendously inspired by Carl Jung's concepts and vocabularies. However, most of the similarities between the books are due to the fact that we are describing the same territory that we experienced in similar ways.

I think *The Journey of Soul Initiation* could be quite complementary to this book because Plotkin talks a lot about vision quests, fasts, and wilderness expeditions as his primary modes of accessing the Below. These have never been part of my own modus operandi and are therefore not prioritized here. However, aside from different practices, I would say that the major difference between Plotkin's book and this one is that his is exclusively concerned with navigating the Below and bringing back elixirs into the Middle. There is virtually no mention of the Above. Therefore, to me, it is a very on-point and extremely helpful description of only half of the story.

Another thing I found electrifying when I first encountered it was Rob Burbea's work on "Soulmaking Dharma." Burbea was a Buddhist teacher and a senior teacher at Gaia House in England, who was primarily known for writing *Seeing That Frees*, an extensive book on emptiness that became a classic among serious Dharma practitioners. Burbea passed away in 2020 from pancreatic cancer. In the last few years before his death, along with his collaborator Catherine McGee, he had started to articulate a new vision that combined Buddhist teachings on emptiness with a Jungian-inspired model of "the imaginal." Unfortunately, he died before he was able to complete much writing on this topic; however, there are a number of recordings of his lectures and retreat instructions available online. This material was extremely helpful to me, both validating my experiences and accelerating my Descent.

To me, Burbea's articulation of Soulmaking Dharma is perfectly calibrated for practitioners who are highly experienced with Buddhist teachings and who wish to start to orient toward the Below. His recordings point listeners who already have some mastery of the Above toward the Descent using Buddhist concepts in a way that I think is quite skillful and inspirational. On the other hand, if you are not that kind of reader, then it will probably not speak to you at all. Another limitation of Burbea's materials, as far as I can tell from the online recordings, is that he walks people right up to the door to the Descent but does not lead them down into the depths. Therefore, it again is an on-point and helpful, although limited, view of the territory. (McGee continues to give retreats and develop this work, and perhaps her retreats go deeper; I don't know.)

A third model that is both relevant and also quite popular in spiritual circles is Adyashanti's teaching on awakening the Head, Heart, and Hara. Personally, I like this model a lot and I think that it has a ton of overlap with this book. I haven't followed Adya closely, but if I'm understanding him correctly, it seems to me that his Head and Heart awakenings correspond to my Above, and his Hara captures some of what I mean by the Below. While his three forms of awakening cover a lot of ground and I have no objection to them, I still feel like there's more to the Below than is articulated in his teaching. To my ears, Adya's descriptions of the Hara don't seem to evoke the darkness, difficulty, terror, and sheer weirdness of my own journey through the Below. Perhaps we could imagine adding an extension onto his Head-Heart-Hara model, a fourth realm located under the Hara, deeper down into the Abyss. (Maybe I'd suggest something like Head-Heart-Hara-Hades, but I don't know if that would pass muster with Adya's marketing team!)

Finally, I wanted to mention one last model that I think is relevant to our discussion here: the one forwarded by tantric Buddhist and Hindu systems of practice. While there are many others, the most well known of these in the contemporary West are Tibetan Vajrayana Buddhism and Kashmiri Shaivism. While I have not engaged in formal training in either, from what I can tell from my reading about them, these two traditions recognize and teach practitioners to work with many of the categories of experiences I outline in this book. (While I have critiqued Buddhism in this chapter as an Above-focused tradition, Tantric Buddhism is an exception.)

Both Vajrayana and Kashmiri Shaivism involve formal instructions for working with the divine feminine, Kundalini and other energies, light, imaginal symbols, dreams, deities, ghosts, and spirits—most of the areas we'll explore in the chapters to come. They each also have a general outline of how spiritual progress is meant to unfold. Buddhist Tantric frameworks, for example, typically begin with practices that prioritize opening the heart and engaging with beneficial deities, then proceed to developing higher states of concentration and nondual consciousness, and then lastly move from there down into the body and the energy system through physical and breathing exercises. In contrast, Kashmiri Shaivism, like other forms of Hindu tantra, tends to incorporate the body from the very beginning.

While the more systematic nature of these Tantric traditions is truly one of the great advantages they hold for many practitioners, this is also, in my view, their principal limitation. Both systems require initiation or empowerment in order to get started, rigorous preliminary practices that go on for years in many cases, and personalized instruction from an accomplished guru. Their teachings are structured, understood, and expressed in a certain traditional way, and deviations from the standard model are typically discouraged or devalued. Moreover, since these Tantric spiritual systems are the products of Indian and Tibetan cultures, teachers in these traditions are not necessarily open to symbolism or practices from other cultures.

These more rigid structures can limit people's ability to participate in these systems if they suddenly find themselves thrust into the Below and need more immediate and more customizable tools. For example, during my own process of awakening the Below, when I suddenly started being visited by Catholic, Pagan, and Indigenous South American deities and spirits, I wondered if a Tantric teacher, although steeped in Asian symbolic and spiritual lore, might be able to help me interact skillfully with the beings I was encountering in their own symbolic and ritual languages. I reached out to a few people with this question, and they laughed at the very idea.

In a way, you could say that what I wound up doing in creating my own synthesis of practices was inventing a DIY version of tantra, so to speak, that resonated with my own unique journey. I needed supportive practices quickly, and this wound up being much more efficient for me than if I had started formal training in tantra at that point in time. It also allowed my awakening process to have a totally unique symbolic vocabulary that reflected my own individual cultural, psychological, and spiritual makeup. (Of course, you might feel differently and prefer the security and structure that established systems can provide over the DIY ethos I am presenting here. If that's the case, then by all means, follow your own intuition!)

One last thing that I wanted to mention about tantra is that I do really like Kashmiri Shaivism's appreciation for the divine feminine. This is pretty much completely absent in all the other sources I discussed above. The gendering of consciousness as masculine (Shiva) and the manifestation of phenomena as feminine (Shakti) is something that makes intuitive sense to me, and the exuberant celebration of Shakti that you find in the tradition matches my own felt sense of things very well. For me, the whole Below has a strongly tangible feminine quality to it. In fact, I almost wrote this whole book referring to the Below as "her" instead of "it." Even though I chose not to for stylistic reasons, for me, I very much see these pages as my own honoring and celebration of the goddess. Someday, I'll figure out how to express what I really want to say about her, and I'll write a whole other book. Meanwhile, although we have other priorities to attend to here, and I may not draw attention to the fact as often as I'd like, please know that the divine feminine is always here, behind every word.

Since I've already mentioned a few books above, let me include a list of a few more resources that may be helpful for people sojourning in the Below. While I learned most of my "DIY tantra" techniques from the Below itself, each of the books listed below provides more detail and tools about various aspects that we will be exploring here. Note that I am not recommending them because I agree with any claims they might make about what's ultimately true. I am recommending them because I appreciate the practice advice that they give. Some of these were published more recently, after my journey was completed, but overall I have a lot of gratitude to these authors and I acknowledge a great debt to them for influencing my journey and my thinking on this topic.

- David Abram, *The Spell of the Sensuous: Perception and Language in a More-Than-Human World* (1996)
- Bayo Akomolafe, *These Wilds Beyond Our Fences: Letters to My Daughter on Humanity's Search for Home* (2017)
- Cynthia Bourgeault, *Eye of the Heart: A Spiritual Journey into the Imaginal Realm* (2020)
- Barbara Carrellas, *Urban Tantra: Sacred Sex for the Twenty-First Century* (2007)
- Robert Falconer, *The Others Within Us: Internal Family Systems, Porous Mind, and Spirit Possession* (2023)
- Daniel Foor, *Ancestral Medicine: Rituals for Personal and Family Healing* (2017)
- Bonnie Greenwell, *Energies of Transformation: A Guide to the Kundalini Process* (1995)
- Julie Henderson, *The Lover Within: Opening to Energy in Sexual Practice* (1999)
- Langston Khan, *Deep Liberation: Shamanic Tools for Reclaiming Wholeness in a Culture of Trauma* (2021)
- Chöying Khandro, *Dakini Journey in the Contemporary World* (2023)
- Matt Licata, *The Path Is Everywhere: Uncovering the Jewels Hidden Within You* (2017)
- Bill Plotkin, *Soulcraft: Crossing into the Mysteries of Nature and Psyche* (2003)
- Bill Plotkin, *The Journey of Soul Initiation: A Field Guide for Visionaries, Evolutionaries, and Revolutionaries* (2021)
- Martín Prechtel, *Secrets of the Talking Jaguar: A Mayan Shaman's Journey to the Heart of the Indigenous Soul* (1998)
- John J. Prendergast, *In Touch: How to Tune In to the Inner Guidance of Your Body and Trust Yourself* (2015)
- John J. Prendergast, *The Deep Heart: Our Portal to Presence* (2019)
- Reginald Ray, *Somatic Descent: How to Unlock the Deepest Wisdom of the Body* (2020)
- Reginald Ray, *The Awakening Body: Somatic Meditation for Discovering Our Deepest Life* (2016)
- Lorin Roche, *The Radiance Sutras: 112 Gateways to the Yoga of Wonder and Delight* (2014)

- Evelyn Rysdyk, *The Nepalese Shamanic Path: Practices for Negotiating the Spirit World* (2019)
- Sarangerel, *Chosen by the Spirits: Following Your Shamanic Calling* (2001)
- Mary Mueller Shutan, *The Spiritual Awakening Guide: Kundalini, Psychic Abilities, and the Conditioned Layers of Reality* (2015)
- Mary Mueller Shutan, *The Body Deva: Working with the Spiritual Consciousness of the Body* (2018)
- Tara Springett, *Healing Kundalini Symptoms: Proven Techniques That Really Work* (2020)

CHAPTER THREE

Descent into the underworld

Awakening the Below is challenging. But let me stress that challenging spiritual experiences are not in and of themselves signs of the Below. Difficulties are faced by pretty much all spiritual journeyers at one point or another. There can be immense challenges that emerge in the Above as the ego-self loses its familiar identity and anchor-points rooting it in the conventional world. There can also be challenges that arise in the process of Embodiment, as someone attempts to integrate their experiences of the Above back into daily life as a human being. All sorts of fear, disorientation, trauma, triggering, wounding, shadow material, difficult memories, and strong emotion can arise as part of any spiritual process. In the extreme, these experiences can share symptoms with depersonalization-derealization disorder, depression, mania, psychosis, and other serious mental health disorders. Difficult spiritual experiences of all kinds can become bridges into the Below, but none of these are indicative of the Below in and of themselves.

A true Awakening of the Below has a distinct pattern. It begins with a Descent. The call to descend may feel like an inescapable draw, magnet, or gravitational force that seems to be tugging at us quite against our will. Or, it might feel like a Siren's cry, a bewitching allure that is simultaneously exciting and terrifying. Or, it might feel like the gentle, warm glow of the earth or the physical body beckoning for us to relax into its soft embrace. Or, the quality of this call may be eerie, strangely dark, potentially even scary or seemingly evil. Or, it might be a literal voice in your head inviting you to enter into a mystery. We might be attracted to the call, repelled, or we might try to ignore it altogether. Particularly if Above-based spiritual teachings have told us to reject or recoil from such things, we might succeed in deferring the Descent for a time (although I'm not sure if you can permanently). Or, we might say yes, not realizing what we're getting ourselves into. For many of us, the Descent will not be a choice; we will just find ourselves thrown into it.

Once we turn toward the call, whether through our choice or not, a chasm will open up and we will be drawn down into its darkness. This process is never a perfectly step-by-step linear one, and everyone's experience is unique. Some people find themselves having dramatic mystical experiences when moving through the Below, while others have more of a gradual unfolding. Some people experience high levels of absorption whereby their entire reality seems to be shaped by the Below to the exclusion of all else. Others are able to maintain a wider, more holistic perspective that allows them to do the work of integration as they go along. Awakening the Above and Below may happen sequentially or simultaneously, or perhaps all mixed together. (For me, it was thoroughly mixed together, but also seemed to oscillate back and forth between which realm was more prominent at any given time.)

Despite these differences in how the Descent occurs, generally speaking, there is a recognizable pattern of further and further deepening into the Below over time, like the sequential unfolding of layers. As you Descend through these layers, the Below progressively takes on a life of its own. You might say that the Below wakes up to itself. It becomes an autonomous power or force that begins to exert its will on our lives and to make demands of us.

Remember that when I say awakening the Below, I am not just talking about having a few brief glimpses of the Below or a few "reconnaissance missions" from your headquarters in the Above. This is an awakening process in which we are drawn or led into a sustained engagement. For an extended period of time, the Below becomes our home. As we acclimate to this territory, we stop trying to reframe the Below in terms of the Above (awareness, oneness, emptiness, etc.) or the Middle (psychology, neuroscience, etc.). Instead, we begin to understand and accept it on its own terms. We become fluent in the Below's language. Our eyes adjust to the dark, allowing us to peer into its mysterious corners. We become spelunkers of its cavernous depths. Eventually, it swallows us up altogether as we fully merge with its depths.

This chapter introduces some of what you can experience while Descending into the Below. These aspects are generally presented here in order of depth, with more profound layers appearing toward the end of the chapter. However, that is not to say that every reader will encounter every layer mentioned here, or in this particular order. Remember that this is only a model meant to be suggestive, not a comprehensively accurate statement of ultimate truth. In fact, I don't believe there ever could be an exact map of the Below because the territory itself is by definition unpredictable. As I've said before, everything I've talked about in this book should be read more as poetry than science.

Imaginal phenomena

For most people, the first clear calling of the Below comes in the form of "imaginal" phenomena, a term popularized by the scholar Henry Corbin. Experientially, his term *mundus imaginalis* ("imaginal world") is referring to a category of phenomena that is distinct from rational thoughts, emotional states, and even mystical experiences of the nondual or heart-opening variety. Despite the similarity between the words, the imaginal world is also quite distinct from the ordinary imagination you might use when daydreaming or playing make-believe.

Corbin offers a description of the imaginal in his article titled "Mundus Imaginalis or the Imaginary and the Imaginal," which is freely available online. Other works that have greatly influenced my thinking on this subject include Cynthia Bourgeault's 2020 book, *Eye of the Heart: A Spiritual Journey into the Imaginal Realm*, and also Rob Burbea's talks on Soulmaking Dharma, discussed in the previous chapter.

I'll be using my own language here in this chapter, but I think all of these authors would agree with me that imaginal phenomena are images, archetypes, symbols, and events that are characterized by strong emotional charge, density of meaning, and transformative power. Imaginal phenomena appear to us as autonomous, independent entities or forces, but yet somehow at the same time are deeply familiar, like they are mirroring parts of our psyche back to us in external form. When unpacked and engaged with, they reveal surprising and subtle connections between different types of experiences and events across time and space. They have an uncanny way of connecting our thoughts, memories, dreams, and other inner experiences with manifestations in the material world. Crucially for our purposes in this book, they are also the most immediate and effective gateways to the Below.

Rather than laying on more abstract descriptions, let me relate to you an example of an imaginal phenomenon so you can get the flavor. My friend Jeff Richards is an artist in Denver, Colorado. His main artistic practice is working with paint and thread against wooden frames to create stunning three-dimensional imagery. He writes a periodic blog called Hexagon Art (hexagonart.blogspot.com), in which he described a mysterious event that took place in his studio one night back in 2022. I've quoted this story below, combining material from two of his posts with only a few minor grammatical tweaks:

> I had been working on a large circular panel, laying out with thread a grid of squares and then painting over that grid with layers of color. Other than the intentional nature of the grid as a starting point I had no firm idea of where the piece was going to go. As is often the case, I was simply content to let the process take me where it wanted. Unfortunately the [artwork] took a wrong turn … A little discouraged, I decided it was necessary to retrace my steps and get onto firm footing. I spray-painted a rich blue color over the entire circular surface, laying the paint on heavy to assure that I would end up with a solid blue color field as my new starting point. It happened to be late in the afternoon and, realizing the thickness of the wet paint would take quite a while to dry, I lay the piece on a work table and packed it in for the day. As I headed out the door I caught a last glimpse of the shiny wet blue circle, hoping with a sigh that the freshness of a new day would indicate a different direction for me to pursue …
>
> Then something I can't account for happened overnight and I returned to discover a masterpiece; a totally unexpected, unimaginably sublime message from some source outside my experience, conscious or unconscious. This was a real, full-on Faerie moment.
>
> I was dumbfounded by the sheer beauty of it, by the absolute coherence that is so evident. A strange feeling of otherness came over me, the sensation that some alien presence had shaped the paint. Even today it looks to me like a symbolic language, an alphabet

with a distinct yet mysterious message that speaks not to the rational mind, but to something deeper, something almost instinctual, something untranslatable, ineffable, yet profoundly moving.

Jeff's description of the blue circle and his reactions to it make it clear that this was an imaginal event. In the presence of the imaginal, we feel dumbfounded, awe-struck, at a loss for words. We feel the presence of something deeply mysterious, even sacred, intruding into our lives from a different realm. Reading the blog, you can feel Jeff grasping for the right language with which to express the power this image held over him—he uses words such as strange, otherness, mysterious, instinctual, untranslatable, ineffable, moving, and sublime. Later in the blog, he settles on "faerie" as a shorthand to capture the bundle of emotions, meaningfulness, and power evoked by the mysterious disc.

Another important aspect of the imaginal that emerges from his blog is Jeff's assertion that the blue circle was presenting him with a "symbolic language." This is a pivotal moment in his engagement with the imaginal. Someone else might have noted the event as a weird coincidence or mystery, and just shrugged and gone about their business. But, Jeff chose instead to accept and engage with the symbolic language of the mystery.

His first thought was to try to recreate the same effect again, and his blog describes his many efforts to reproduce the series of accidents that led to the creation of the masterpiece. However, after much trial and error in vain, Jeff writes:

> It occurred to me that I was approaching this conundrum from a completely wrong perspective. It wasn't a matter of identifying causal factors, like solving a chemistry problem. There would be no solution for me at the end of a physics equation. The real truth was that I needed to figure out how to communicate with the faeries; and to do that, I might have to translate the message in the artwork.

This last observation is key. In imaginal phenomena, often an alien or autonomous entity brings a message from beyond this world. Whether big or small, this message is felt to be a mystery—something that needs to be unpacked and explored. But, this exploration cannot be done in a methodical, scientific way. As Jeff suggests, the rational mind is the wrong tool for this job. The imaginal speaks to us on a wholly different level; it calls for a different part of us to come forth. What's important is not explaining or understanding imaginal phenomena, but rather engaging with, coming into relationship with, and opening up to them. It's not about figuring it out: it's about deepening the connection.

Jeff's experience of the imaginal came in the form of the spontaneous appearance of a mysterious object, which called him to enter into a conversation with entities or powers he calls faeries. However, imaginal phenomena need not always take such concrete material form. It may be a mysterious event, say a synchronicity or an especially meaningful interpersonal encounter. It may be a specific place, person, or memory. It may be a dream that leaves a particularly powerful impression. Images, symbols, figures, landscapes, animals, words, abstract geometric shapes, numbers, body sensations, smells, sounds, flavors—nearly anything can appear with the strong emotional charge, density of meaning, and transformative power that are the hallmarks of the imaginal.

I said above that imaginal phenomena can also reveal connections between different types of experiences and events across time. Jeff's blog doesn't get into that particular aspect of the blue circle. But, I know from talking with him that it appeared to him to have a certain futuristic quality, as if the faeries were broadcasting messages back in time. For me, on the other hand, my imaginal world often takes on a historical tinge. If the blue circle came into my imaginal world, for example, I might have been tempted to describe the different patterns in the painting as a message written in an ancient runic script.

Imaginal phenomena often bend time altogether, collapsing past, present, and future together. The same symbol may contain multiple resonances with ancient mythology, with something I remember from my childhood, and with events or people in the current day. As I engage with this symbol over time, more and more resonances emerge or are revealed. Deja vu and synchronicities will emerge that bring these facets further into focus. Bit by bit, as this mysterious presence is unpacked, its significance deepens. Eventually, what started out as a discrete event becomes what Jungians call a "personal myth," a complex story containing deeply felt truths about my life and my place in the cosmos.

Do you notice how the imaginal is inviting us down further into the Below with all of this? The imaginal is not Transcendent. It's not about moving up and out of the mind and psyche, or about leaving the individual human condition behind. On the contrary, it's about moving down into the deeply felt and deeply personal. Although they seem to come from beyond and have an alien feel, imaginal phenomena connect with our own personal past, present, and future and with our own personal set of symbols and meanings. The imaginal thus is a bridge to the deeper, unconscious layers of our self: down into the Below.

The imaginal is not exclusively associated with the Below, as there are entire imaginal worlds associated with Above traditions. Actually, you might say that one of the most significant roles that myths and symbols play in Above-based religions is to envelop the practitioner in an imaginal world of sacredness, holiness, goodness, and light. Catholicism's vocabulary of symbols, to take one example, includes a whole range of angels, saints, Jesus, Mary, and other figures that can be very alive for someone as teachers, guides, protectors, and messengers of the sacred.

However, while Catholicism accepts and embraces these particular figures, it simultaneously rejects, vilifies, and demonizes the darker side of its own imaginal vocabulary. While some parts of the imaginal world are sanctioned and thought of as good, others are to be avoided and thought of as sinful or evil. Figures such as Satan or images of Hell are treated as anathema to spirituality. This same move is made in other Above-focused traditions, such as we saw with Mara and his daughters in the myth that opened this book.

Contrary to these examples of Above-centric traditions, one of the most notable things that is happening when awakening the Below, in my opinion, is an awakening of the darker side of the imaginal world. Those aspects of the imaginal that have been walled off as dark, sinful, unwanted, or evil begin to stir and to emerge from the shadows. The imaginal phenomena associated with this kind of Awakening process can seem exceedingly dark, or a blend of both light and dark, depending on the individual.

While it may be disconcerting if you have internalized the taboos against the dark side of the imaginal, there's nothing innately wrong with it. In fact, there are many religions worldwide that have long embraced it. From Asian traditions, think of the wrathful deities such as Mahakala and Palden Lhamo from Tibetan Buddhism, or the dark goddesses such as Kali and Durga from Hinduism. Think of Hades, Hecate, Circe, and Nyx from ancient Greek and modern Paganism. In Celtic tradition, there's the Morrigan, or Aophis from Egypt. None of these traditions eschew or reject these dark entities, and I personally have found that researching such traditional figures is one of the best ways to validate, unpack, stimulate, and engage with my own imaginal darkness.

Those who engage with the dark imaginal often find it to be just as exquisite and impactful as the light. By way of example, let me relate an imaginal experience had by my good friend, Jack Morrígan, a spiritual teacher, healer, and long-term explorer of the Below, who has taken the name of the Celtic goddess. (All of the stories I am quoting in this book without mentioning a particular source were provided to me by email or orally, and are presented here with some minor edits to condense them or make them fit with the book's flow.) Jack recounts:

> The Morrigan is my primary deity, and she's a deity of death, sex, and magic. Once, I remember her coming to me in one of her forms, in which she has a raven's head and long, claw-like hands covered in feathers, and blood all over her mouth. That might look horrendous to someone else, but to me, I know who she is. I love her. So what I feel looking at that form is love and sexual attraction.
>
> And one time—almost like in a waking dream—she bites into my wrist with her beak and pulls out blood and muscle, and she connects it to her wrist, and she says, "Your blood is my blood is your blood." And I feel this flowing energy, like my body being purified spiritually through my blood by this deity that I love.

If, like Jack's, your own imaginal world is tinged more darkly than typically allowed by the Above-based traditions you're familiar with, you might recoil from such a visionary experience. You may find yourself thinking that such dark imagery has no place in a spiritual process, that all visions should consist of divinity and light. The incongruity between your expectations and the realities of your visions may produce confusion, fear, or shame. But, in truth, you have no control over what your imaginal world looks like, and there's no predicting it in advance either. So, you might as well open up to it and see what there is to discover in the darkness.

I already mentioned that when my own imaginal world opened up, it took me completely by surprise. Having been steeped in Buddhist and Asian religious imagery for my entire adult life, I was perplexed when a completely different range of symbols and entities suddenly started emerging. It turns out that my personal imaginal landscape includes a whole spectrum from light to dark. On the lighter side, figures like the Virgin Mary, a radiant Pagan sun goddess called Sol, and the Buddhist goddess of mercy Kuan Yin all play major roles as protectors and guides in my visionary experiences. But there is also a whole pantheon of darker animal spirits who embody more primal sensations. A black jaguar who protects me when I journey into dangerous territory, a vulture who eats the parts of me that I am ready to let go of, an owl who facilitates encounters with ghosts and wandering spirits. In fact, the most significant figure of all, who I'll introduce in more detail below is a goddess who is half angelic and divine, and half serpentine and demonic. I also experience a multilayered imaginal realm that has expansive upper regions with vast landscapes of mountain ranges and jungles, as well as a cavernous underworld with networks of catacombs and dark lairs. Different guides and protectors inhabit different parts of this realm, and I travel in visionary experiences to visit and converse with them in their different locations.

That's the way the imaginal shows up for me, but as I've said a few times already, there's no reason that you should think that any of my experiences—or Jeff's, or Jack's, or anyone else's I'm mentioning here—are normative. The point is to discover, embrace, and enter into relationship with your *own* imaginal world, whatever it might be like. Light, dark, nurturing, or scary, all imaginal phenomena have important messages for you if you engage with them and invite them into a relationship. Aside from surrender, this kind of active engagement is one of the most important core skills of navigating the Below. For as we'll see, the Below is saturated with the imaginal all the way down, and all of it is inviting you into relationship.

Energies and spirits

That autonomous or alien quality—how the imaginal feels like an external agent when it manifests to us—is going to be a common theme as we move forward. Because they are not part of the everyday ego's understanding of the self, most of the aspects of the Below are perceived as external forces or entities, things that are appearing to us and having an effect on us, rather than being part of us. This perspective can be heightened for people who have already experienced a significant degree of attenuation of the ego-self due to nondual experiences or some of the other realizations that can be found in the Above. In other words, the less firm your grip on the ego-self, the more you may open up to experiences that seem to be coming from beyond you.

We can experience this sense of "beyond the self" in the form of abstract external forces or as independent entities such as spirits, ghosts, demonic beings, or past lives. In Jack's story in the previous section, it was clear to him that he had experienced a visit from a goddess named the Morrigan. In Jeff's story, the situation was more ambiguous. Was the blue circle created by a disembodied intelligence that Jeff is calling "the faeries," or was it made by individual faeries who he understands as discrete beings? Or maybe, was the artwork itself the faerie, a living being with autonomous agency and a voice of its own? Jeff doesn't get into any of this in depth in the blog, but how he, or Jack, or any other person experiences imaginal phenomena doesn't matter for our purposes here. What's important is how *you* experience them.

When encountering the more difficult aspects of the Below, people who experience them primarily as impersonal energies often talk about nebulous feelings of oppression, darkness, black clouds, malevolent forces, and so forth, while those who experience autonomous beings will talk about demons, ghosts, dragons, or other fearsome spirits. On the brighter side, "energies people" speak of lights, colors, auras, and energy fields, while "entities people" speak of angels, devas, dakinis, and other spirits of light and radiance. Whether seen as energies or entities, these phenomena can be imaginally charged with all of the emotion, meaningfulness, time-bending, and transformative qualities already mentioned.

What's ultimately going on here? Are we discovering various autonomous aspects of the unconscious, as Jungians would argue? Are we uncovering a collection of protective and wounded "inner parts" as they might put it in Internal Family Systems? Are we engaging with independent beings that are wholly external to ourselves, as most Indigenous worldviews would say? These different systems might be interesting to research and may offer helpful tools and insights. However, ultimately, our opinions on the question of what's actually going on don't matter. Remember Jeff's dictum that this is not a physics equation we must try to solve. What's important is that these energies and entities are calling us to engage. Whatever they are, we are called to come into relationship with them, to communicate and translate their messages, and to deepen our receptivity to them.

To illustrate, let me share with you two stories about learning to engage with energies that were initially experienced as uncomfortable, but then opened up to become something special. The first one comes from my friend Lisa, who shared with me how she discovered that she needed to surrender to what felt like an immensely oppressive energy in order to find liberation from some limited ideas she was carrying about herself:

> I feel this journey has been around the theme of surrendering to the feminine in myself. To allow it to be there. To nurture it and honor it. But in a completely different way than I have ever known or had been taught. I had to go into the depths of the ugliness, face the traumas that took place, and to be stripped of everything around what I thought it was to be a woman.
>
> I am still only just coming out of this process, so I have no idea what it all means, but this feels incredibly important to my journey. And it was so scary and painful to go through at points because it felt like I was giving everything of myself up. Everything that gave me any joy or security about myself, it had to go in order for this process to take place. I can see how this could be seen as a "letting go" process that's typical of awakening experiences, but it just feels different in that it was incredibly painful at points and certainly did not fit into the other awakening experiences I was hearing my peers talk about.
>
> I felt stripped of absolutely everything I had. I continuously found that any attempt I would make at trying to make myself feel better about myself or my appearance was not able to be fulfilled. I couldn't muster any energy towards putting on make-up or working out. All the things I used to do that would bring me some sense of self-confidence were just not possible in this condition.
>
> It felt like I had no choice in the matter. I couldn't will myself out of this process. I had to let it take over me. I had to give myself to it. I had to face the depths of this space, to be it, to become it, and to rise out of it in its own time, when it would allow me to do so.

In the second story, my friend Jack discovered that a destabilizing energy he sensed in one of his clients actually had a valuable lesson for him:

> One time, I was working with a client and she had an intense energy. It was a traumatized energy that I didn't feel I could handle. I'd have sessions with her and I would worry that I couldn't hold

that space. And then afterwards I'd have to lay down and I'd get this weird experience where I felt like the ground from underneath me was like being taken away. It felt very unstable, and it would make me anxious.

One evening, I lay down on my bed after one of these sessions with her and I just decided that I would accept what was happening. It felt weird, but the more I relaxed into it, the more comfortable it became until my body felt like it relaxed. And through that, there was a kind of rootedness. I felt rooted more into the earth and relaxed into a more expanded state of consciousness. It was like, through the intensity of her energy, she was initiating me into a deeper level of expansion within myself.

The common theme in both Lisa's and Jack's stories is learning to open up rather than seeking to explain or understand. Like them, I also had to overcome my own ideas and preconceptions in order to establish a working relationship with the seemingly autonomous forces of the Below. I am decidedly an "entities person," and initially, for me, accepting that fact was difficult. Very soon after my Descent began, I encountered a large number of spirits who emerged to me in rapid succession. Each one seemed to be calling for my attention, for me to speak with them and receive their messages. By this point in my life, I had adopted a more rational, skeptical viewpoint toward spirits, ghosts, and other paranormal phenomena. Accepting what was happening at face value seemed to go against the identity and self-image I had built for myself. ("I'm just not that kind of person," I told myself.) The more numerous and more insistent on speaking with me these entities became, the more anxious and unsettled I felt about all of it.

All of that came to a head one day when I suddenly remembered that I voluntarily became possessed by spirits when I was a teenager. I had invited them to take over my body during a Lakota Sioux power animal dancing ceremony, and I remembered feeling exhilarated and empowered by the experience. I had been closely involved in sweat lodges and other aspects of Lakota ritual for several years when I was a teenager, which I remembered well, but I had for some reason completely blocked out the episode with the power animals.

Next, I remembered that as a child of about seven or eight I used to perceive inanimate objects as discrete spirits, and have conversations with them all day long. I had also blocked out that memory. Putting the pieces together, it suddenly hit me that I was imagining myself as a skeptic, but I really was holding spirits at arm's length because I was afraid. Afraid of what it would mean if I admitted to myself that I believed in them. Specifically, I realized that I was afraid that opening myself up to the spirit world meant that I would be opening myself to black magic, attacks by demons, and other nefarious influences. In other words, I wasn't a skeptic at all; I actually believed in spirits deeply and, in fact, always had!

That realization was a turning point in my relationship with the spirit world. From that moment onwards, I began to invite the spirits I encountered into a more intimate relationship. I'll talk more about some of the techniques I started to incorporate in order to establish communication and deepen the relationship in the next chapter. What's important for the moment is to emphasize that—whether we see the imaginal world as energies or spirits—the more we engage with it, the more it will open up to us.

Even when we decide we are willing to work with energies or entities, sometimes our first reaction to them is colored by preconceptions or misapprehensions that we need to overcome in order to receive the messages that are being offered. For example, my friend Jack discovered that a deity he initially perceived as dark and scary was actually wanting to nurture him:

> Kali was the first spirit or goddess of the underworld that I really connected with consciously. And it happened because I was going for dinner with a friend at an Indian restaurant, and my friend pointed out all of these images of Kali with decapitated heads that were everywhere. She was like, do you know who that is? That's Kali, goddess of death.
>
> And then maybe a week later I was walking through a park and I opened myself up to Kali just to see if she was there, and I felt her energy come in. Initially her energy was very intense, frightening almost, like she was screaming and shouting. But, then I felt her sending a message from her consciousness into my mind: "No … I'm Mother Kali. Mother Kali."
>
> What she explained to me was that my mind had taken these images that I'd seen and projected an idea that this deity was intense and frightening onto her. And she was coming in to correct that misinterpretation. I was filtering her message incorrectly

42 AWAKENING THE BELOW

because of my preconceptions, so she corrected me. And, my welcoming her in the form that she wanted to be with me created the start of a relationship that has evolved and lasts to this day and is one of the most significant relationships I have with any being.

When we begin to engage and understand spirits and energies on their own terms, instead of through our preconceived ideas about them, they begin to open up. As more imaginal phenomena come forth, our perception of them becomes clearer. A lexicon of symbols, images, events, energies, entities, and other imaginal elements begins to coalesce. A mandala or network or landscape begins to take shape in which all of these elements stand in relationship to one another. The more we explore this world, the more connections will emerge between these nodes, reinforcing and enriching each other and revealing further messages.

As we learn the topography and features of our own personal latticework of spirits and energies, we will find our own place in this imaginal web and begin to more confidently navigate its complexities. We will discover that certain aspects of the Below are here to offer protection, others to guide us, and still others to provide valuable insights about how to create boundaries or clear away negativity. As we develop fluency with this matrix of energies and beings, we find ourselves able to engage in two-way communication with the Below. We can ask questions and receive teachings and guidance. We'll come back to discussing specifically how to do this in the next chapter. For now, let's keep moving deeper on our journey of Descent.

Autonomous bodily intelligence

Another place where a sense of autonomy and alienness emerges—sometimes to our great surprise and consternation—is in our relationship to the physical body. On any spiritual journey, our relationship with the body tends to undergo radical transformations. In the Above, for example, the body is one of those things that we Transcend beyond. In fact, disidentification with the material form through the realization that "I am not my body" is often one of the first things that propel people into this trajectory. As nondual realization dissolves the subject–object division, we see that what we thought of as "the body" is a mere collection of sensations floating around within awareness—or appearing within a void, depending on your flavor of nonduality. As a deeper level of nondual deconstruction takes hold, those body sensations also are seen through. The body dissolves into tiny particles of energy that barely can even be said to arise at all. As the quality of divinity comes to the foreground, this empty and insubstantial body can take on the qualities of pulsation, bliss, joy, and divinity. A "body of light" or a "rainbow body," as they say in some traditions.

Moving into the Below is a totally different story. In the Below, the body is not transcended or dissolved. Rather, it comes alive as its own autonomous intelligent being. Again, there's a difference between those who experience this intelligence as an energy or impersonal force and those for whom it is a personified entity. For the former, there is a knowingness, wisdom, or felt sense that the body somehow seems to possess, quite autonomously from our mental apprehension or perceptions of it. This autonomous intelligence asserts itself spontaneously, taking control of the awakening process, healing old wounds, and activating, energizing, and balancing out the energetic system. Here is how a friend named Misha BearWoman Metzler described her experience of this process:

> I wake up most nights two hours after I went to bed. I feel a particular energetic quality, a kind of arousal or activation that's been going on for years. I've joked with friends that this is "life having its way with me."
>
> I'm in a liminal state. I feel intuitively guided to engage in different ways. The body begins making spontaneous, organic, symmetrical movements that are dancelike. My hands move into very precise, mudra-like postures. I vocalize, though not usually in words. I might tremble or shake. I may find myself pressing hard on areas of blockage, such as the throat or liver. From the outside, these things might look like possession. From the inside, I'm opening, expanding, clearing, releasing, healing, awakening.
>
> I find myself doing energy work with and on my body, encountering and resolving psychological issues. Waves of emotion may arise, need to be felt, expressed, released. I sob away old hurts. Chakras or other energy centers may activate, energies may move around in a multitude of ways. Many kinds of spiritual experiences and insights occur. At times it's like the deep phase of a psychedelic journey. Sometimes sexual energies arise and I engage with those.

> Generally, I just stay very receptively present and notice what happens or wants to express. Sometimes I use some of these periods to listen to recorded meditations or dharma talks, or feel guided to go outdoors and bask under the night sky. Nowadays, even if I'm not paying full attention, whatever process wants to happen just happens anyway.
>
> An episode might last between ten and ninety minutes, or sometimes even longer. When several occur in a night, which is more often than not, there is generally a progression in the processes that occur. The last round generally begins about an hour before dawn.
>
> These experiences feel purposeful and directional. Even when I can't recall precisely what shifted, progressed, or resolved, I can feel beneficial differences in my being.

I can totally relate to Misha's experience, and something quite similar happened to me on my journey through the Below. However, people who are more attuned to entities, as I am, will likely also experience the autonomous intelligence of the body as a distinct creature with its own agenda and will. The spiritual teacher and healer Mary Mueller Shutan calls this the "body deva" (deva means a spirit or a deity in Sanskrit), a term that I feel is quite apt in describing my own experiences.

I met my body deva during a Kundalini event that kicked off my initial Descent into the Below. When Kundalini arose, it felt like my whole body was taken over by a serpentine goddess. Over the course of the next year, I kept having visionary experiences of this entity: a feminine form that was half serpent, half human, with dark, black, scaly coils below and radiant sunshine pouring out from her head above. When she appeared, she would often enter my body and begin to move me around. She would teach me qigong-like sequences combining breathing and visualization. She would use light and energy to heal and empower my body.

This goddess became one of the primary entities in my imaginal lexicon, a powerful symbol that I felt was speaking to me at a visceral level. And, for all of that time, I took this entity to be a goddess that was wholly external to me. However, eventually, this goddess revealed herself in a powerful visionary experience to be none other than my own body's inner consciousness. From that point onwards, she no longer felt alien or like she was "taking over." Rather, this goddess became the symbol or icon for my own body in my imaginal world. Working with her in this way, she became so closely associated with my experience of my own body that it's now entirely natural for me to experience my physical body as this goddess.

In whatever way it manifests, whether as a relationship with an intelligent energy or an entity, in a Descent, the quality of the interactions between you and your body are of the most intimate nature. In order to engage in this relationship, what the body needs is for you to hear and accept its deepest truths. It needs you to give it the space and time to tell you about its memories, traumas, and wisdom. The whole time that your ego-self has been deeply identified with the body, it has ignored, walled off, and repressed these uncomfortable truths. The ego has repeatedly told the body that it needs to be quiet, to shut down, to deny parts of itself, in order to be safe.

In the process of awakening the Below, as the body begins asserting its independence and autonomy, the ego-self often has no choice but to place aside its preferences and allow this communication to take place. What the body reveals when it is listened to can be crushing to the ego, and this unburdening process can for many be one of the most difficult areas of the Below. Eventually, though, you learn to meet the body with loving patience and acceptance, without ego-identification or the impulse to recoil. You hold it in a loving embrace and allow it to speak its truths no matter how difficult. You learn to surrender to the process, and to allow the body to express itself, and through this, to heal itself.

Here is how Lisa experienced this kind of opening:

> Right from the start I had to give my body over to this process. This body, as I once knew it, was no longer mine. A few days after my initial transcendent awakening experience, where I was shown I was pure light and was visited by both God and Jesus, my whole body exploded internally, releasing all the pain and trauma that was stored in each and every cell.
>
> This pain contained traumas that I had known, traumas that I thought I had already worked through and resolved, and traumas that I had absolutely no memory of. I remember thinking, I cannot believe a human body could hold so much pain! How could such a thing actually be possible? I went from someone who was incredibly active, always moving, going to the gym, going on hikes, always engaged in active projects, cleaning and cooking and stretching and moving, to someone who couldn't even walk down the street due to the insurmountable emotional pain I felt in my system.

> I had to descend down into the depths of my shadows. Allowing myself to be taken over by a sense of pure ugliness and disgust. Memories of awful experiences from childhood and thoughts of any harm that I have ever experienced over the course of my life surfaced. I found myself wanting to hide any aspect of beauty or attraction from the world. I was cloaked and clouded in ugliness, in an aura of dullness. My life went from somewhat difficult but certainly enjoyable, to entering into the complete depths of this inner darkness.
>
> I knew on a very deep level from that point forward my only job was to surrender to this pain, allowing it to consume me completely. My body was no longer mine, there was a much bigger process taking place now. Something far beyond what my own mind could understand or try to control.

While it can be excruciatingly painful at first, over time, a foundation of trust builds. The body goes from being a source of shame, disappointment, and disillusionment to being a deep well of groundedness and intimacy. It goes from feeling alien to feeling like an old friend and companion. There is a sweetness to the energy that is shared between you, like between two old lovers who have been enamored with each other for decades.

Sexual energy

As the body wakes up to its own agency and power, one of the things that invariably occurs is that sexual energy, which has long been bound up and controlled by the ego, is unleashed. Here, as with the other happenings discussed throughout this chapter, the ego-self's reaction is often to desperately try to force the genie back in the bottle. Sexuality is a topic of particular concern for the ego—often wrapped up with a great deal of trauma, self-loathing, shame, blame, and other emotions that can make this particular territory difficult to navigate. I'm afraid that my brief comments here are going to make this topic sound much more straightforward than it actually is.

Like with other aspects of the Below, sexual energy liberated from the control of the ego is experienced as an alien or autonomous thing. Like with other aspects, it can be experienced either as an impersonal force that wells up uncontrollably, or as a wholly independent conscious entity. In an experience of the former, the journeyer may be overwhelmed by floods of sexual desire, imagery, or behavior that are much stronger than previously experienced or that are directed in ways that one is not used to.

Here is how one friend of mine, who wished to remain anonymous, described how her sexual energies woke up and began to move autonomously in her body. This friend has a long history of trauma, including childhood sexual abuse, so healing has been an essential component in her awakening process:

> After a period of concentrated work, I experienced my heart opening energetically, emotionally, and relationally. I also experienced resolutions in psyche- and body-based imprints and holding patterns. Part of this healing and awakening process was a deep opening of my natural sexual energies. Though years past menopause, I found myself engaged in periods of daily masturbation—sometimes several times a day, or even closely spaced together.
>
> Although there is much more sexual arousal than there used to be, orgasm is a much more energetic experience for me now. I no longer get the physical rush that I used to. There is physical pleasure, but it's different from before. At first, I found that the energy dispersed into an expanding energetic field. Sometimes, the energies drew into the dantian spontaneously. Other times I felt guided to draw the energies elsewhere, or they went somewhere (in or near my body) on their own.
>
> One night as I was lying down masturbating, a new thing happened. My intuitive sense was to focus on the energies above my pelvis. I felt them as a deep gray swirling whirlwind of moist air. Reaching the threshold of arousal, the energies spontaneously dropped down, entering my body and moving around in organic ways. Some went to my left lower abdominal area. The majority swirled to the right side, then up (through and past some of the digestive organs, including the liver), and continued swirling over to my heart.
>
> I trusted the process, allowing it to happen as it would. Afterwards the areas those energies moved to felt more healthy, whole, clean, and pristine. Since then my sexual experience has increasingly become energy-focused. Often the attention is solely on where the energies want to be focused and build. There are no fantasies of any kind, and it's more like the process is driving itself and I'm simply a willing partner in that process.

For those who experience autonomous entities, on the other hand, it may be that they perceive their own sexual energy as an actual being that is separate from themselves. This being may appear in visions or dreams, or may be a felt presence in waking life. For me, as a person highly attuned to entities, during the Descent, I experienced sexual energy in the form of a radiant goddess. She appeared in a form that captures everything I find most attractive. I would often experience her walking beside me, hugging me, or just appearing before me in my mind's eye.

During my sojourn in the Below, there were enormous surges of sexual energy, and these would always be accompanied by a visitation from this angelic spirit. Just her presence alone would set off a flood of orgasmic feelings, waves of bodily bliss and pleasure throughout my whole organism. These would be visual as well as tactile experiences, where it truly felt as if I was with another human person in the most sacred and liberating embrace. It took me a long while to recognize that she was actually the externalization of my own sexual energy and not an entirely independent being.

While I personally experienced a feminine figure, sexual energy might take on any other kind of shape. Listen to Jack again, as he tells the story about his interactions with his primary spirit guide, who used her shapeshifting power to liberate his previously repressed sexual energies:

> At first, the Morrigan would come and visit me regularly, say how much she loves me and that she wanted to initiate me into a tantric relationship across dimensions. And I could feel her passion for me, and I felt it for her, and we had this really loving relationship that was also very sexual and primal.
>
> She is very playful, and she would be like, "I can look like whatever you want me to look like. I can be whatever you want me to be. I have no limitation." So, she would present herself to me as all of the things that I find the most attractive. Including things which I've been suppressing through my life, such as the homosexual side of myself.
>
> She would come to me, part man, and would be interacting with me. And that would be something that I knew was turning me on, but that I was afraid of as well, and she knew that, so she would hold it sensitively. It's like she was unearthing the sexuality that she knew was inside of me, because she held no judgment toward it whatsoever, and loved all of this within me.
>
> I wasn't ready for that in my life, but she helped me through these experiences, which later led to me having my first homosexual experience. I remember afterwards I felt such an enormous relief.

She knows what's in the underworld and can show it to me in ways that help me to feel safe with it and even live it in my life. To become part of my freedom.

As Jack learned, what the body wants is to free itself from all sexual inhibitions and hangups. The ego might fight against these developments mightily, and kick up all kinds of resistance and emotions that will need to be worked through. In the end, though, all repressed preferences must emerge from the closet, and any unresolved trauma must be faced and given voice. Ultimately, the autonomous bodily intelligence wants to express itself and heal through the medium of pleasure. It wants to bathe itself in freedom and bodily ecstasy. It wants to fall in love with itself, to experience the utmost intimacy of the tender, warm, and erotic embrace between energy and matter. The body can do none of that while the ego-self is in charge.

The specific ways that the body wants to love and heal itself lie completely beyond the ego-self's ability to control or manage. The ego might want us to be straight when our body wants to be bisexual, or cis when we're trans; it might want us to avoid certain sexual activities when our body wants to engage in them; or it might be using sexuality in order to forward its own egoic ends that are completely at odds with what our body actually wants or needs.

In the process of awakening the Below, the body deva is going to wake up and assert its autonomy over all such things. The ego will resist, and there will be conflict and suffering, but eventually we will learn to surrender. The process may be completely lovely, as it was for me and my anonymous friend above. Or, completely liberating, as was the case for Jack. Or, completely overwhelming, as we'll see in one of the case studies in Chapter Five. Or, it may be completely destructive, leading to divorce or other kinds of upheavals in your life. The awakening of the sexual energy of the body is completely unpredictable, and thus it is one of the most dangerous aspects of awakening the Below, needing great care, sensitivity, and ethical attention to navigate.

Ancestral materials and past lives

As we deepen into the Below, we continue to peel back successive layers of the onion. Thus far, the aspects we have discussed have mostly pertained to one's individual life—one's own lexicon of imaginal symbols, energies, and spirits; one's own body and sexual energies; one's own personal traumas, hangups, and issues. Sooner or later, however, the trajectory descends down beyond the individual biographical material, into the deep past. Here, we are getting down into levels that are structural, the scaffolding that lies underneath one's own personal stories.

Once again, this material can come forth either in the form of impersonal energies and forces, or as discrete entities. For example, ancestral material is often experienced as a thicket of intergenerational trauma, racial trauma, or issues related to culture and heritage that need to be untangled. Alternatively, it can be experienced as visitation from the spirits or ghosts of specific ancestors. In the case of past life material, the journeyer may experience feelings, memories, emotions, or other phenomena that seem to come from previous incarnations; or, they may be visited by a previous self, or experience becoming that previous self for a time, seeing through those eyes.

For me, a major part of my experience of the Below was what I would call ancestral trauma. My late grandfather had a difficult upbringing in Colombia, and we were never allowed to speak to him about his family or background. But, late in life he revealed to a family member that he was half Chibcha, an Indigenous group from around Bogotá. That's about all I knew about that side of my family heritage, and to be honest, I hadn't thought about it in much detail or looked into any information about the Chibcha or other Indigenous Colombian people.

But, when I had that Kundalini event where the serpentine body deva revealed herself, one of the things I did to try to understand what was happening to me was to research serpent goddesses. Naturally, I started with Asian goddesses in order to see if I could find an image that matched the description of the one I was experiencing in my visions. I had a clear image in my mind's eye of what I was looking for. I found a few images online of Kundalini, Nagkanyas, and other Asian serpent spirits, as well as Echidna from Greek mythology, but nothing was fitting perfectly.

Then, one day, I had a visionary experience where again I saw this goddess, but also some other imaginal symbols—a jaguar, an Indigenous person's face, a waterfall in a jungle. This made me think to look for a serpent goddess associated with indigenous South American cultures. A fraction of a second after typing a few Spanish keywords into Google, I found myself breathlessly staring at the exact image I had been seeing in my mind, a statue called "Bachué, diosa generatriz de los chibchas" (i.e., "Bachué, Mother Goddess of the Chibchas") sculpted by the Colombian artist Rómulo Rozo in 1925 (see Figure 3).

Figure 3. Bachué, diosa generatriz de los chibchas, Rómulo Rozo, 1925.
Source: Wikimedia.

This image of Bachué would become the single most powerful symbol in my journey through the Below, the organizing image of my entire imaginal world, and my principal spiritual teacher. I already mentioned that this goddess is none other than my body deva. What's significant to emphasize here in this section about ancestors is that, although you might expect that such a tremendously impactful image would have arisen from one of the Asian religions I had spent such a huge amount of my life studying and practicing, it arose out of my ancestral heritage, even though I knew next to nothing about that culture.

Once I knew that this image was coming from my Indigenous roots, this part of my heritage opened up for me a great deal. In the succeeding months, I began to experience more and more imaginal phenomena related to South America. Over those same months, through a series of really astonishing synchronicities, I also came into possession of photos, ID cards, and other memorabilia from my Colombian grandfather's parents and grandparents—people whose very existence was never allowed to be mentioned in my family. My heritage was coming alive, and was intervening as an autonomous force into my life!

However, as my Indigenous ancestry came more into focus, the portion of my DNA that comes from European settlers in South America did as well. Catholic imagery became much more pronounced in my imaginal world, connected with both my maternal and paternal side. Now, I found myself imaginally reckoning with what felt to be a conflict between two different sides of my own genetic code. I experienced visions of the genocide of one side of my ancestry perpetrated by the warfare and violence of the other. The details of how those visions played out and how they came into resolution are a story for another time. For now, I just want to reiterate yet again how important it is to engage with the imaginal symbols or images. The more interest you take in them, the more you allow them to unfold and reveal deeper and deeper resonances.

An alternative type of experience of ancestors that I also want to draw out here is how individual ancestors can allow you to see through their eyes or inhabit their bodies in a kind of time-bending experience. I'll turn it over to Jack again for a story about this kind of interaction with his grandfather:

> I was in Marseilles traveling with my partner at the time and we went on a small boat to go to one of the islands off the coast. It was

the first time since I'd started to awaken that I was on the Mediterranean Sea. My grandfather, my mother's father, was in the British Navy, a commander of a destroyer during the Second World War, and his ship was sunk by German U-boats in the Mediterranean, and he spent three years as a prisoner of war.

And, when I was on the sea, I suddenly started getting these images flashing into my mind from the bridge of a warship. It was like I was looking through my grandfather's eyes, and feeling what he was feeling.

And through his eyes I saw this little speck on the horizon on the sea. And then I saw a flash and I realized he had just seen the guns go off on an enemy warship. And it was his first time that happened and he froze and was so afraid, because he realized this isn't a simulation anymore; this is real. That's actual artillery fire from a warship firing at my ship, and I'm responsible for the lives of all of these men. And I remember the fear, and the shock and disbelief.

But what it's done is helped me understand him and what he went through and the way that his experiences, the fear that he had, have been a part of my own life. And through connecting with him I've been more able to release that fear. It's good; it's cathartic for me.

The kind of catharsis Jack is describing can also come through experiencing past lives. In Above-based spirituality, the emphasis is normally on releasing the trauma or karmic burdens of past lives so that the individual soul can become lighter or more spiritually evolved. In the Below version of past life recall, as always, the emphasis is not to transcend or release but to welcome and fully embody the past, so that it can become liberated to express itself in the here and now.

Here's my friend Kini describing her encounters with one of her past lives, who emerged as a guide in her shamanic journeying and soul-retrieval practice:

> The only way I can describe it is that it was like a spontaneous download. I got this full packet of information about this past life of mine as an African shaman who was very stocky, and strong, and kind of low to the ground, and powerful, very grounded. And I got his name, Umkumbe, his history, and even how he died.

> This was just spontaneous. I didn't reach out, I wasn't looking, but it just came as a download. I knew he was a guide, but I also knew he was me in a past life. There was a sense of support and grounding, in part because he was so solid. He also had white ash on his body, which was like he was shielded or protected in some way.
>
> Umkumbe has been with me ever since. He's my shamanic guide, and when I go to do work in the underworld, for myself or for clients, he's there and supports me and whatever work I need to do, and he'll heal or guide. I'll go down into the underworld through a hole in a tree at a specific place where I grew up, go down the tree trunk into the earth, and come out in the underworld. And he's always there with his cloth laid out and implements, and I'll sit down with him. And he'll present me with objects or situations that I must navigate in order to learn a lesson.

Whatever way ancestral and past life materials manifest, what is wanted is a full accounting of all the ways that our being has been shaped by deep history. It turns out that the ego, which has always thought of itself as the master of its own destiny, has been wrong about that. As we learn to welcome, communicate with, and remonstrate with ancestors and past lives, we come to see how little of our present lives have ever been under our control. We come to realize how events long past continue to shape our present experiences in ways that have been invisible, unappreciated, or even denied by the ego. We find out that our genetic and karmic inheritances have given us both blessings and burdens, and realize the steps that need to be taken in order to receive the former and rectify the latter.

Working to unearth, appreciate, and fully embody all of these structural influences allows us to walk through life with a confidence and self-composure that is liberating. A sense of completeness that can only come from thoroughly knowing and understanding the makeup of our being. There are no hidden skeletons in the closets, no shameful secrets we hide from ourselves or the world, no historical wrongs or injustices that we aren't fully owning and inhabiting.

We will also likely experience our work in the Below being deeply beneficial for the whole chain of ancestors and our previous incarnations stretching out into the past, as well as for living family members and children yet to be born. While I was working with my ancestral material, for example, I saw visions of an infinite web of relations, stretched out and interconnected with one another like a vast fishing net. And I saw me stitching and mending this net, retying its frayed ends and washing it clean to restore it to its original vibrant colors, revitalizing this network of ancestral support and connection for all my relations across time and space.

Animals, nature, and the elements

Peeling back yet another layer of the Below, we discover that underneath our cultural and genetic heritage there are even deeper layers of unconscious structure, the biological and the elemental, that also want to awaken. Here, all of the same principles we have been examining will come back into play again, just at a deeper level.

There are many spiritual teachings from the Above that speak of the interconnectedness of nature; the evolutionary process of Gaia; the way that all of life is continually developing toward greater self-awareness, wisdom, and enlightenment. Once again, the insights coming from the Below are not contradictory to those from Above, but complementary as they are oriented in the opposite direction. While the Above approach is to see how individual organisms are ultimately all part of the greater processes and divinity of Gaia, the Below approach finds nature to be filled with individual, autonomous forces and entities with will and agency of their own that need to be expressed.

These forces and entities can be associated with animals, plants, cellular, or subcellular life. Or, it can be the whole complex living system of all biological life and organic materials across the planet. Or, the planet itself. Or, the solar system, galaxy, or entire living cosmos. Or, they can be the elemental particles that make up the cosmos—traditionally thought of as the elements of Earth, Water, Fire, Wind, and Space, but in modern times just as commonly conceived of in terms of the periodic table we learned in chemistry class. Any or all of these might come alive when awakening the Below, intervening and communicating with us through imaginal events, imagery, symbols, or in synchronicities, or directly in words.

To give an example of the apparition of autonomous entities, here's my friend Lisa talking about being visited by animal spirits of various types. She has discovered that they always have lessons or wisdom to share, if only she is able to engage with them and let them do their work:

> I would sometimes be visited by giant snakes that would take over
> my body and slither through my subtle energy field, helping to

strengthen and heal any contracted energy points in my system. They would protect me and unravel blocks of trapped fear. Large wild cats would take over and dance through me, teaching me to strengthen myself and feel strong in my body when I have to stand up to others or stand in my truth.

I have learned a lot from these visitors over the years. They would always leave after I fully allowed them to come in and take over my body, when the lessons they came to show me were fully understood. When I would fully allow the process to take place, it always felt like the right thing to be doing in that moment. It felt like a complete alignment, like this is fully what was meant to be happening. I could feel my nervous system strengthen and afterwards I would feel more whole in myself and in my body. They offered me this transformational gift with each and every visit.

One memorable example was when, at the start of this whole process, I found a teacher to work with, but after a short period of time of being with her, I started to get strong hints of intuition that working with her was not very helpful. I could sense deep down that this hurt and traumatized body needed a softer and more loving approach than she had, but didn't quite know how to find that just yet.

During this time, when I was alone by myself wondering what to do, a snarling protective dog came to visit me. It took over my body, barking and growling through me. It was pointing its energy at her image in my mind, as if to keep her energy away. It was protecting me. When I allowed this process to happen and I received the wisdom of this animal, I knew I had to step away from this teacher, to find someone else to work with. The spirit dog pointed me towards my own inner knowing and helped me to believe in my feelings and my intuition. Once I fully heard the message the dog was sharing with me, it disappeared.

Encounters with nature often blur the lines between the imaginal and the material world. Listen to my friend Misha recount how her relationship with spiders developed on both sides of this divide:

> During the past six years of my awakening process, spiders have been repeated visitors, and my relationship with them continues to deepen. I delight when spiders come to visit with me, and I feel

especially charmed when they're exhibiting atypical spider behavior. For years it was the domestic house spider. There was the one who kept visiting at my table when I was in a months-long experience of intense love and divinity, going so far as to crawl on multiple occasions onto the journal I was using. There was the one who gave its life, sacrificing itself willingly like Jesus on the cross, at the center of a rug in the threshold of a doorway I used frequently, "so that I may live." That was an experience of redemptive love. This past fall, a jumping spider showed up for several weeks. How delightful!

Imaginally, a beautiful black spider with a large furry abdomen and equally long legs recently showed up. I undertook a sequence of five related inner journeys, and she showed up repeatedly then. The first journey involved a huge amount of purging on many levels, which extended for about twenty-four hours. At one point, while I was on the toilet with another bout of crying and otherwise releasing, she came up very close to my face.

I leaned backward onto the physical support of the seat cover, toilet tank, and the wall behind, letting myself immerse into the whatever it was that needed to be known and felt before it could move on through. As my body was twitching and multiple orifices were releasing their bodily fluids, and as my emotional heart was bleeding and I was re-experiencing the chaotic disorganization of a shattered psyche, Spider suddenly tightly grasped my entire head in her many legs. Her body was pressed up against my face. I was fully embraced in her Love.

This was such a profoundly moving experience—to be held so firmly and tenderly during this difficult and exhausting experience—that just recalling this kind, loving hug now, I cannot help but be moved to tears.

Both Lisa and Misha talk about being visited by animal spirits, but another kind of realization is to experience your own conditioned existence as a human animal. Perhaps you experience that your body deva or bodily intelligence has attributes that are animal-like, or perhaps you feel various animalistic urges and energies surging within your fleshly body. Perhaps you feel the mammalian urges to seek warmth, to bond, and to feel a sense of belonging in a community. Or the urges common to animals of all types to feed, procreate, and survive. Coming to know some of your behavioral or emotional patterns as expressions of these natural animalistic energies helps you to allow them to autonomously exist and naturally express themselves within your being without shame, judgment, or resistance.

Another thing we can realize and experience is how our bodies are also homes for entire communities of autonomous beings that are not part of us. Scientists estimate that there are about 39 trillion bacteria, viruses, fungi, and other microbial cells that live on us and in us, outnumbering the 30 trillion cells that make up our own bodies. This leads us to ask how much of "us" is really "us" in the end? We can, for example, come to understand how our microbiome is expressing itself through food cravings and digestive processes, our general levels of immunity and vitality, or our mood. Each one of those alien cells has its own genetic inheritance and its own agendas beyond the control of the ego.

Descending even further into the microscopic, we can also experience how we are conditioned at the molecular level. How do hormones like testosterone and estrogen dictate what we think, what we feel, and how we behave? How do neurotransmitters, cortisol levels, and other aspects of the body's biochemistry drive and shape every moment of our lives. Beyond the molecular is the layer of elemental conditioning, where we can find the powers and energies of the natural elements at work within our bodies and minds. Each of these can potentially be experienced as its own consciousness or entity exerting autonomous forces on us.

Tapping into these aspects of nature can be powerfully transformational. Perhaps I'll illustrate this by relating a story from my own experience about the time I visited the Niagara Falls. If you have never been there, this is truly a wonder of the natural world. This massive waterfall sees 3000 tons of water, or nearly 700,000 gallons, passing every second. I did not expect that standing on the edge of the falls would be such a visceral and overwhelming experience. The deafening roar of the water seemed to shake the ground, my body, and my entire being.

At that point, I was well into my Descent and had a lot of experience with entities and energies, so I responded to this power by asking the falls to come into a dialogue with me (see the next chapter for this kind of technique). I found that relating to water in this way was different than speaking to entities such as animal spirits and ancestors, who have a more individual presence. It was like I was meeting the full force of the elemental nature of water, an impersonal but enormously powerful energy. It was not a dialogue of words, but rather of sensations.

As I opened to feeling the immense power of the sheer volume of water, letting it in and surrendering to its sensations, it felt like a downward torrent of water flooded through my torso as all of the energy in my body flushed downwards. It was like there was a drain in my perineum, where the rushing water fell down into a bottomless chasm. It was an intense visceral experience, but it also felt both purifying and healing. It felt like the falls were teaching me something about the way the energy of water worked within my own system.

In time, I learned that this teaching from the Niagara Falls was a tremendous gift. It helped me to learn to tune in to a downward flush of energy in my abdomen whenever I feel ungrounded or scattered. It's now become something as automatic as muscle memory. I can just exhale once, and the whole energy in my torso drops down through that drain in the bottom, leaving greater relaxation and balance.

My experience encountering the power of the elements concentrated at a particular natural site like the Niagara Falls is not unique. If you are interested in reading more stories specifically involving engaging with the wild and learning how to cultivate a relationship with its imaginal power, I can heartily recommend Bill Plotkin's book *Soul Initiation*, which largely focuses on these types of energies and entities.

The bottom line is that, in the Below, rather than Transcending nature, we come to experience ourselves as intricately enmeshed in a web of relationships with all sorts of natural energies and entities. We also begin to experience our own bodies as inseparable parts of nature. We are in relationship with all of the other aspects of nature that make up the planet we live on, and are intricately tied to all of its environments and ecosystems.

These deeper animalistic and natural layers of conditioning lie underneath the mental, emotional, biographical, and even ancestral levels. We may have learned a number of scientific facts about these deeper biological and material structures, and we may be used to thinking about all the ways that they are interconnected parts of Gaia. But in the Below, we can also experience encounters with these as autonomous forces and entities. While Above-based traditions emphasize Transcendence of the natural world and the evolution of Gaia in the direction of increasing spiritual virtue, here in the Below we invite the whole of the material and animal world to come forward as it is. We welcome it all—sublime grace and bloody violence alike—every grain of sand and every molecule of water—to become alive, to manifest in our lives, and to speak their authentic truths. By being welcomed, these aspects are all liberated to join in the process of our awakening.

Here's a quote beautifully capturing this sentiment from Jack's first interview on the Nonduality Podcast by Nic Higham (as usual, slightly edited):

> It's like a descent from this heady witness consciousness down into the heart, and into this really open loving consciousness that united me with humanity. I felt this descent almost like the roots of a tree going down. And it feels like it's just gone down into the heart of the earth—and this is where it's really difficult for me to talk about this stuff without crying, because it gets so intimate and personal—but it's descended into Mother Earth.
>
> I can feel her spiritually, and it's a difficult thing to describe, but it's almost as if I can feel a void open beneath me, like a spiritual void of awareness, that just goes down into her and we have a relationship like that. We're connected through our spirit, and it's so intimate and supportive and wonderful. I know I'm her child. This isn't an idea that I'm trying to think up; I know that as a spiritual experience, something that I feel.
>
> And that sense of unity consciousness where I look at another being and it's like I'm looking in the mirror—I get that when I look at trees and when I look at mountains and the water. I know that I'm looking at the greater part of myself when I look at those things. And to me, they aren't "things." To say that is kind of blasphemous, because those are beings, and I love them. And I have a very intimate connection with them and they teach me. I feel like I am just a part of them, and I am just trying to catch up and learn what they've known for a long time. And they are teaching me.

Seeing the Above from the Below

As mentioned in the previous chapter, awakening the Below is a different process than awakening the Above. Each has altogether different insights, experiences, and goals. Moreover, different people may have different experiences with the relationship between Above and Below.

Some people will be thrust into the Below and will become completely absorbed there for a time. Others will feel like they are oscillating between Above and Below or intertwining or blending the two together. As I mentioned previously, the latter was very much what happened to me. It was only after profound nondual awakening experiences that my Descent began. Consequently, the perspectives and insights I had gained in the Above always informed my experience of the Below and vice versa. In fact, for me, both Above and Below were fused together in ways that are difficult to separate out after the fact. I am only isolating Above and Below as relatively separate realms or processes for purposes of clarifying what's distinct about the Below in this book.

With all of that in mind, here in this section, I want to give you a sense of how the Above can look from Below. In the first place, you should know that it's entirely possible that, at least at times, the detached transcendence of nonduality (of either the self-as-awareness or loss-of-self variety) is completely shattered. It's quite common to experience a kind of self/other relationality returning when you're in the Below, through which you relate and engage with all of the imaginal forces and entities we've been exploring. So, for example, even though you have clearly seen that there is no separate self, you may still find yourself engaging in dialogue with bodily intelligence, sexual energies, spirits, ancestors, and others in a second person ("I" and "you") mode. Or, even though you have significantly dissolved your perception, you still may find that imaginal phenomena have a vibrant, tangible sense of reality. Or, even though you have in the past experienced deep peace and equanimity, you may now not be able to find a detached position from which to engage with the Below; everything may seem genuinely sacred, or terrifying, or both.

The important thing to emphasize here is that nothing is wrong. Your awakening is not lost; you're not backsliding; there's no problem to fix. On the contrary, the process of Descent and your sojourn in the Below actually represents a deepening of your spiritual path. For some unknown reason, you are one of the chosen few who have the opportunity to awaken both the Above and Below. If you haven't yet finished your work in the Above, you'll get back to that in due time—whether tomorrow or in a few years. For now, you will need to focus on learning a different skill set to be able to work on the portion of your awakening process that lies in the Below. It may truly be inconceivable from where you sit today, but you will eventually see the Descent and the Below as equally valued and equally inalienable parts of the awakening of your whole being.

While you are down here in the Below, you might continue to experience qualities of the Above and even may see accelerated growth in those areas. For example, insights you gain from dark imaginal phenomena might deepen your appreciation of divinity or open-heartedness. In my case, all kinds of dark imaginal entities enveloped me in fields of radiance and love and taught me how to access aspects of the Above.

To give you just one example, as I was exploring the ancestral burdens and gifts of my paternal grandmother's line, which traces from South America back to Spain, I felt a lot of sadness and loss. But, I also felt a gentle loving presence that gave hope and solace to generation after generation of women in this lineage. As I was communicating with these female ancestors, they revealed to me that this presence, which they had cherished and passed down from mother to daughter for over a millennium, was none other than the Virgin Mary.

A routine part of how I interact with ancestors is to ask them if there is anything I can give to them or do for them. When I asked them this question, this group of women collectively asked me to honor the Virgin Mary. They explained that their intergenerational transmission of Mary's blessings had been interrupted by my late grandmother, who had lived a completely secular life, and they wanted me to revive this connection.

This was a difficult thing they asked of me. At this point in time, I had no interest in Christianity, least of all praying to Catholic deities. But, I also I knew enough at that point in time to take into consideration anything asked of me by my ancestors instead of just saying "no." So I did it. It so happens that there's a major international Marian shrine right up the road from my house, and I went up and paid a visit. I bought a small devotional pendant, and brought it home. I wasn't sure if I was going to actually use it on my altar or just keep it in a drawer, but I was willing to try to engage at least once with what the ancestors were asking of me.

Anyway, to my surprise, the very first time that I called upon Mary in my morning practice, I felt such a strong presence of divine love and protection that I have never turned back. The Virgin Mary (who I, like my grandmothers, call "María") immediately took her position as the principal manifestation of love and protection in my imaginal world. A few years later, I even made a pilgrimage to the Vatican City and bought a decent-sized sculpture of her that has a central location on my altar today. Most importantly, through engaging directly with the figure of María, I have learned from her various techniques for invoking her loving qualities and imbuing my life with them through a brief daily ritual. She has remained a nearly constant presence in my life since that time.

So, that's one example of how a teaching from the Below can directly lead to greater engagement and connection with the Above. Another kind of experience that is worth talking about is what is in neo-shamanic circles called "dismemberment." This is an experience where you imaginally undergo death, either in order to metamorphose into a new type of being or to learn your place in the cosmos. In a true dismemberment, you feel utterly torn apart both energetically and emotionally. Here's an account Jack told me about a highly emotional visionary experience he had with a past life, in which he underwent dismemberment:

> It's funny because there's a part of me that rationally can't believe that this is true, this memory. But every time I speak about it, I almost inevitably burst into tears telling this story. My body feels it so deeply. These memories are very vivid. I remember it very clearly and I remember the emotions connected to it as if it's my own experience.
>
> I remember in a previous life being the high priestess of a community in Celtic Britain and the responsibility of that, knowing that what I say is going to change what happens to everyone in my community. And I know these people and I love these people.
>
> Knowing that the Romans were invading and had been brutally murdering people in neighboring villages, I went to the woods to perform a sacrifice for divination to find out what I should do. There was this deer that I loved and I could communicate with it telepathically. It had agreed to be sacrificed for the good of the community. So, I killed this deer that I loved feeling so grateful, so much love for this deer. And I did this divination using its organs and blood and found that the best course of action would be for me to turn myself over to the Romans.
>
> So I did that, and they took us, and I remember being burnt alive at the stake. (I don't know if that's actually what the Romans did to Celtic priestesses, but that's how I remember it.) And, as I was dying, I remember feeling so sad. It wasn't for me; it was for my community. I felt like I'd let them down, I'd failed, and it felt awful.

> But, then as I was dying, the spirit of Gaia entered me, and I knew so completely that every single thing that was happening was for Gaia's evolution, for my evolution as a living spirit of this planet. And that I and all of my community are Gaia, and that all of the Romans committing these crimes against us are also Gaia. And the sense of separation between us completely disappeared, and I entered a state of deep peace, because I knew that nothing was wrong, and everything was happening for love.
>
> And then I died in the body, but my consciousness expanded out into the infinite. And, I saw Lord Shiva as this huge golden deity, so magnificent. And he held out his hand, and in it was a golden orb. And when I looked into it, I understood the nature of creation. That the entire universe is this masterpiece of threads of life, and that I myself as an individual being am one of these threads, and that I'm contributing to this masterpiece that is so incredible. I can't even put it into words, it's so beautiful.
>
> And I knew right then that no matter how many times I would have to suffer and die, I would continue to reincarnate because I'm doing it all for the most incredible thing that's ever been made.

I was also dismembered numerous times by all kinds of imaginal phenomena, spirits, and energies. Invariably, the experiences were difficult in the moment, but powerfully transformative in the end.

Another frequent occurrence in the Below is for imaginal imagery, symbols, and/or body sensations to indicate to you that your "job" or your "mission" is to stitch together the Above and Below into some kind of balance or synthesis. In my own imaginal world, the image of my body as the goddess Bachué—half radiant, half demonic—serves that function. For Misha, it was seeing herself as a winged being:

> I was in human form and I had wings extending outward to the sides in the basic shape of a Christian cross (my religion of origin is Episcopalian). Though they were stylized, I knew these were my angel wings. The wing on my left side was a dark black, and the right wing was a bright white. Each shone luminously bright in its own way. Each numinously expressed divinity. These wings/forces were equally present, potent, and balanced, just as my human and divine elements were.

My body was in a twisted posture, with the left hand reaching upward toward a bright glowing orb. My right foot was reaching downward toward the darkness, earth, and the sphere of the unknown. I had a distinct impression of God's posture in Michelangelo's *The Creation of Adam*; with each limb, I was reaching out to touch the Divine. In a way it felt yin-yang like, but with much more complexity and subtlety than the classic yin-yang symbol evokes for me. My dark side was reaching upward to touch and absorb into the transcendent emanating Light; simultaneously my light side was reaching downward to touch and root into the rich mysterious depths of the Dark. This was such a potent image of unification in multiple dimensions that I felt drawn to execute it as a full-sized painting.

Another possibility is that imaginal phenomena might even give you direct teachings about nonduality. One day, deep into my Descent, I was doing my usual meditation walk through the neighborhood when I passed by a gruesome scene. A group of men were cutting down an entire line of thick pine trees at the edge of someone's property. Were the trees sick? Were they just unwanted? I didn't know, but I had a sudden strong feeling of sadness and compassion for these fallen beings. As I walked by, I made a point of walking up to the truck and placing my hand on the largest of the tree trunks that were stacked there. "May you be well, grandfather," I said to the fallen tree. "And all of your kin as well." I continued on my walk, my hand smelling of pine sap.

About an hour later, as I ended my walk and night was falling, I took a walkway near my own house. I'd lived in this neighborhood for about a decade, and had used this path before, but it had never struck me in quite the same way as it did on this particular evening. Cutting in-between two houses to enter the shadowy path, I passed through what seemed to be a tree-lined gateway, which gave me the impression I was crossing a threshold into a consecrated area. Then, in the dimness ahead, I saw a circle of eleven trees arranged in a ring around a thick old oak, kind of like they were assembled for a sacred ritual. My imaginal senses fired up, and I felt that something important was about to occur.

As I approached the ring of trees, it seemed that the old oak was calling me to come close and join the circle. I did, and I noticed that there was a stump in the ground, a thirteenth tree that had been cut down. The oak invited me to stand on top of the stump, facing inward toward the center of the circle, and to take my place in the coven. I stood there, a guest among the tree folk, for as long as I could as the moon rose and the stars came out. I could have told you this story back when I was talking about nature and animal spirits, because I was acutely aware in that moment of how hard it was for me, in this animal body, to stand still for such a long time. The trees were showing me that they had infinitely more patience and stillness than I did. As I finally gave up, I thanked them for this lesson and turned to leave, and they invited me to return in the future.

I made a point of passing by that grove every day for the next few months. Each time, I would stand on the stump, stilling my body and mind, and staying as long as possible. I also started sitting at the base of the oak for a while as well, just to continue to savor the stillness even after I could no longer stand. Over those nights, the ring of trees started teaching me to do what they called "listening like a tree."

As I sat listening to the sounds of the rest of the world passing by with all of the energy and movement of "unrooted" animal life, something happened to my hearing. I experienced the dissolution of sensory phenomena. Sound broke down into a stream of tiny particles. Eventually, I saw that those tiny particles of phenomena were not actually particles after all. They were like minuscule energy packets that imploded upon themselves before they even took shape.

Over time, I would lean closer still and learn to apply these insights not only to hearing but to all the other senses as well. Listening like a tree, seeing like a tree, feeling like a tree, thinking like a tree, and so forth, I would soon experience how the whole of reality appears to be fizzing in and out of existence every nanosecond. How each moment is born out of and disappears back into the void so fast that it never really happens in the first place.

The point of this story is to give an example of how the Below can teach us about even the subtlest aspects of the Above. The trees in that grove gave me the crucial insight into nonduality and the emptiness of all phenomena, escorting me right up to the very top of the journey of Transcendence. (Come to think of it, maybe I'll have to rewrite that story about the Buddha yet again, centering on the wisdom of that tree he was sitting under!)

The Abyss

The Below can be exquisite, mesmerizing, ecstatic, and thrilling. But, it invariably will include many moments of difficulty, confusion, and fear. The further into the Below you go, the more pronounced this will become, and at the deepest layers, you will find an all-pervasive existential terror. Typically, journeyers will approach these depths, experience intense fear, and back away into safer territory, repeating this pattern multiple times. The ego spasms in sheer horror each time you approach because it intuits what lies at the bottom of the Below: the Abyss.

Here, let me introduce another quick visual schematic (Figure 4) to illustrate how I'm thinking about this. Like in my discussion of Figure 2, I want to draw your attention once again to the parallel between the trajectories of Above and Below. Each one is a mirror image of the other. Both involve the death of the ego, here indicated by the zenith and nadir points I call the Void and the Abyss.

Contemporary Western spiritual seekers are quite familiar with this process the way it is explained in Above-based spiritual traditions. They know that Transcendence involves an ascent into realms where

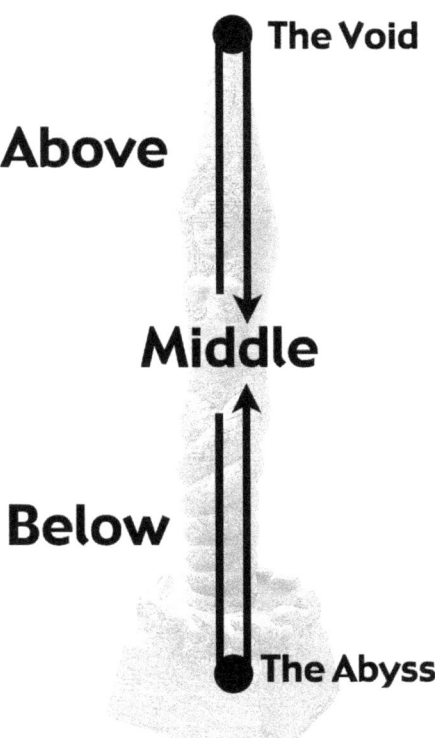

Figure 4. Two portals to ego-death.

the ego-self becomes less and less central, until it is gone beyond altogether. This journey can involve a great deal of fear, as the separate self hangs on for dear life to its familiar identity. Eventually, though, the fear dissolves away as the journeyer passes into the Void, the portal at the loftiest height of the Above. Here, there is the complete falling away of both subject and object, the cessation of all phenomena, the crumbling of any notion of a stable ground upon which anything could stand. You can't even say it is complete nothingness, because the distinction between nothingness and somethingness ceases to exist. This is the culmination of the Transcendent trajectory. The truly indeterminate nature of the universe manifesting on a moment-by-moment basis is finally revealed.

While ego-death from Above necessarily involves going beyond the self and everything it identifies with, the journey of Descent into the Below is moving in the opposite direction. Here, there will also be an ego death, but an upside-down one. Down into the self instead of up and out of it. Down into all the parts of the psyche that have until now lain unconscious.

As we Descend, we peel back successive veils to reveal all of the components that make up the whole of our being: the psychological wounding, the deep traumas, the protective and obstructive forces, the gifts and burdens, and all of the other aspects and influences that have sculpted our personalities and our bodies and our lives. In awakening the Below, we are not focused on witnessing, or holding in awareness, or clearing, or integrating these aspects. Rather, we are learning to totally liberate these aspects from our control: to fully allow these parts of ourselves to reclaim their autonomy, so that they can come alive and wholly express themselves.

As the Descent proceeds, we come closer and closer to the ultimate test. In the Abyss, we will be challenged to endow with autonomy and freedom and to allow to come alive and fully express itself nothing short of our deepest, darkest, most secret, most core fear. We will be challenged to not only unleash, but to fully embrace, the very thing that we have ignored, pushed away, papered over, and denied our entire lives. Every cell in our being will reject this and recoil in horror. We will beg, plead, and pray for it not to be so. We will try to fool ourselves into thinking our journey is complete, declaring ourselves done and trying to begin the Return prematurely. Anything to avoid falling into this Abyss!

I was contacted by Misha at precisely this moment in her Descent. She described being on the precipice of the Abyss as follows:

> There were episodes when it was as if I were sliding down the inside of a smooth-sided funnel. I was sliding inevitably toward some narrow aperture, with who knows what on the other side and nothing to break or slow my fall. It was like I was free-falling through open air. And I was frightened of when I would hit the bottom, which I viscerally imagined would break me.
>
> As I approached the threshold, it felt terrifying. I kept grasping for anchor points, the old tried-and-true techniques I'd learned to do during years of meditation practice. In fear and anxiety, I would reach out for one of those trusty old friends, and after a brief contact it would dissolve and run out of my hand like sand. Sometimes as I was reaching for these previously reliable strategic practices, they even evaporated before I could touch them.
>
> How could my hard-won helpers not be working!? As they disappeared one by one, I'd start feeling frantic. What was I to do? Where was help to be had?
>
> Eventually during one of these episodes, I desperately called into the unknown: "Help!" And help did come. Now it was as if that funnel were completely lined with overlapping hands, each of which was clothed in a soft, silky white glove. I literally felt these on my body as I was going through this experience. None of these gloved hands stopped or even slowed my fall. But their presence did gently caress me (in a passive way) with kindness and care as I passed.
>
> In some way, that touch was reassuring. It felt like even though there was no other kind of intervention forthcoming, a caring presence was somehow letting me know it was there with me. That wasn't my last free-fall, but at least I had something that helped.

In Misha's account, we can see some of the most common features of the Abyss. The notion of a dark tunnel or hole is frequently mentioned, as is the sense of loss of control, the sense of the unknown, and the fear. Pretty much everyone employs all the strategies they know when approaching the Abyss, desperately looking for someone or something to hold their hand as they fall, or to catch them on the other side.

In my case, my first encounter with the Abyss happened early on, within the first few weeks of the Descent. I recoiled in horror, primarily because I feared that going through the Abyss would mean loss of my sanity. Over the next two years, as a whole range of imaginal, spirit, bodily, energetic, ancestral, and other changes took place, I kept periodically reencountering the Abyss and recoiling in fear. Toward the end of that period, these encounters were coming more and more frequently, and it became apparent to me that the time was coming when I would have to be swallowed up.

I knew from all my time in the Below that surrender was the key practice, and I knew intuitively that this would be the only way to face the Abyss. But, try as I might, I could not wrap my head around letting go of control. In increasing desperation, I prayed to Bachué, María, my other goddesses, my power animals, and my ancestors on a daily basis. Both to help me surrender and also to help protect and guide me into and through the chasm that lay before me.

But, alas, it could not be so! The pull of the Below is like a black hole whose gravity is inescapable as it devours everything. This is the ultimate dismemberment. The ego must utterly die, and there are no strategies it can use to steer you through this portal while remaining intact. All of the tactics and "helping hands" we have relied upon to feel safe as we approach the Abyss must eventually be let go of. The ego has learned to surrender as ever deeper layers of the Below have woken up and become liberated from its control, but now it's time for even the most subtle of the ego's habitual strategies and safety mechanisms to utterly fail. When the moment comes that we are finally sucked away into the Abyss, we have no choice but to make that transit naked and alone.

In more ways than one, the Abyss is a birth canal. And, rest assured that it will be a birth. But first comes a very real death. And, just like when the body passes away, the only thing our guides can do to help us when that the precipice comes is to encourage us to let go. This is how Jack's guides helped with some tough love at that crucial moment:

> I felt my spine rotating backwards to an impossible degree, and there was a snap. And there was just darkness. In the distance, there was a point of light, and it started getting brighter and larger. As it got larger, I felt this orgasm rising inside of me. And I also felt an existential terror that I was going to be destroyed on a fundamental level. This is it! This is the actual end!

It just got more and more intense to the point where I felt like I was screaming, like I was falling off a cliff and I was about to hit the rocks. There was a threshold, and then some kind of being appeared and invited me to cross over the threshold. I said no, because I thought I would be annihilated if I crossed.

And then it lovingly gave me a little push!

Coherence

What lies on the other side of the Abyss? What could you possibly find at the heart of a black hole of infinite darkness? Well, when you finally totally surrender to the thing you have feared the most and allow yourself to die, a most astonishing and profound transformation takes place. This is at once the deepest mystery of the Below and also the simplest thing imaginable. Spoiler alert: it turns out that the thing that your ego has always feared the most is exactly the elixir that, all along, your soul has been called to gather up.

It has always been so. This has been the central tension throughout your entire life: you have unconsciously been pouring an enormous amount of energy into denying, repressing, holding at bay, and otherwise ignoring this existential terror. But, when you finally accept the Abyss and allow it to fully consume you, you realize that behind this terror had always lain nothing less than the very destiny that your entire life has been preparing you for and that your entire being has been perfectly designed to fulfill.

To put it bluntly, you realize that what you have always been deeply, utterly terrified to accept is the fact that *the elixir is actually you*.

Of course, I don't mean that the elixir is the ego-you, but I also don't mean it's just the part of you that is awareness, or your heart, or your higher self, or any other specific part of you. The elixir found in the Below is the whole of you, every level and layer of you, including all the virtues and kindness and open-heartedness, of course, but also all the traumas; all the wounds; all the unconscious aspects of your psyche; your physical body and its energies; all the decisions, successes, and disappointments in your life story; and all the hidden ancestral, karmic, natural, and material structures all the way down to the very last atom.

When you Transcend through the Above and into the Void, you experience ego death because you go beyond all reality and even consciousness itself ceases to exist. Ego death is totally different in the Abyss.

When your ego dies in the Abyss, every aspect of your whole being is completely present. The death of the ego allows these parts to autonomously heal themselves. It allows them to become relaxed, undefended, and liberated from all that controlling and micro-management. All of it can now be awake and alive and vibrant, for the first time free to actually be the elixirs that they all along have wanted to be.

What word can we use to capture all of that? Plotkin speaks of "soul initiation," and I personally love that term. Yes, to me, the awakened wholeness of your being can indeed be called the soul, and the transit through the Descent and down into the Abyss for sure is an initiation. But, because both of those words have a lot of other connotations and are used in various different ways that could be confusing or off-putting for some people, let's just use a neutral term like "coherence" instead.

I call what lies beyond the Abyss coherence because, once you have been initiated into the totality of your awakened being, the entire journey through the Below, no matter how difficult, is seen to always have been perfectly orchestrated to arrive at this exact moment. All the puzzle pieces fit together into an exquisite picture, and everything turns out to have been both necessary and completely worth it. All of the imaginal phenomena, spirits and energies—even all the drama and terror around the Abyss—snaps into alignment. Or rather, they are all revealed to have been in perfect alignment with the soul's plan all along.

I mentioned earlier that, during my own Descent, I had approached the Abyss many times over the course of two years, and that I had repeatedly recoiled from that precipice in fear. As the experiences came more and more frequently, I prayed to all of my guides for help and guidance. I also reached out to my good friend Jack. By this time, he and I had become quite close through sharing the details of our spiritual experiences and giving each other support and advice. When I asked him how he dealt with the Abyss of terror that lurked at the bottom of the Below, in typically Jack fashion, he responded with the advice to lean in and embrace the darkness. "Just reach down into that chasm," he said, "pull up all the terror you find down there, and spread it to the four directions, surrounding yourself in a sphere of fear."

It sounded to my ego-ears like exactly the worst advice imaginable, but early one morning not long after, as I did my predawn meditation, I resolved that the next time I found myself at the edge of the Abyss I would do exactly what Jack had said. After meditation, I felt sleepy, so I took a nap before continuing with the rest of my practices.

While I slept, I had a distinctly imaginal dream. For many years, I had different versions of a dream where I am pulling on a string that goes down my throat into my stomach. As I pull and pull on that thread, mucus and bugs and various other nasty things come out from inside. That morning, however, for the very first time, I came to the end of the string. With one final tug, something deep in my abdomen released and there was a sensation of deep visceral relaxation. I immediately awoke.

Feeling that this was a good omen, I continued with my morning practice of drum-assisted visualization. Practically as soon as I closed my eyes, the Abyss was there before me. Like many others also report, I experienced it as a deep black tunnel located at my perineum. The Abyss felt like a chasm of fear underneath me, a roiling ocean of terror upon which no stable ground could possibly be found. Specifically, it was fear of madness and annihilation—and, deeper at the core, fear of loss of control.

So many times in the past, I had arrived at this precipice and had recoiled, but this time I felt I was ready. With Jack's advice still fresh in my mind, I decided I would reach down into the black hole and unleash the darkness. In my visionary mind's eye, I placed my hands down into the depths. My physical heart was pounding and every cell in my body was telling me to run away. But, I simply accepted and surrendered to whatever was about to happen.

As my whole being screamed in terror, I grabbed a handful of the darkness and drew my hands up to "place it in the four directions" around me, as Jack had advised. But, as I opened my hands, I made the most astounding discovery of my life. I found I was holding a golden, liquid light with the quality of the most profound and divine love imaginable.

I must have done something wrong! I reached down again into the Abyss, looking for the darkness, trying to grab ahold of the terror that had been so menacing, but each time I pulled up my hands, there was nothing in them but radiant love, all the way down. I realized in that moment that the terror the ego had felt about going mad and being swallowed up by the Abyss was always just love in disguise. I realized that all the machinations of the ego had been due to the love my being had for itself, for my family, for life, and for the world. I realized that all of it—every last bit of suffering and pain I had ever experienced—was always just another face of love. There never had been a problem in the first place! I burst out laughing at the absurdity of it all, as a wave of bliss shot through my body and lit up my scalp.

And just in that instant, I saw the form of the goddess Bachué. Like in every other vision I had ever had of her, she was wearing a mask of tranquil equanimity (see Figure 3). But this time, she took it off and revealed her true face underneath, which I recognized as none other than my own brilliant soul.

Seeing that vision, everything snapped together at once. Until that moment, I had been relating to all of the aspects of the Below that I have been describing here in this chapter as separate entities, spirits, deities, and forces. But, now, like a series of Russian matryoshka dolls nested one within the next, they all clicked together. I knew in that moment that all of the guardians and protectors, the power animals, the angel of sexual energy, the body deva, and all of the higher imaginal beings and goddesses with whom I had been communicating throughout my sojourn in the Below—all, without exception—were part of one single, multifaceted being. It was also clear that all of the ancestors, past lives, natural forces, and structural elements, as well as my own personal biography, were all parts of this being as well.

All of the aspects of this multidimensional being cohered into Bachué's body, with each piece of the overall puzzle assuming a different location within her form. This whole assemblage then merged with my body, and the brilliant golden light of my soul, Bachue's true face, flooded the whole system. It exploded out of the top of my head, creating a blazing mandorla of radiance and bliss around me.

Now that it's been several years since this coherence event, I can attest that my ego has come back on line a million times since that day. But that is perfectly okay, because now I know that, despite all its fumbling and bumbling, it too is made of love. And, also, it no longer believes it's in charge. Astonishingly, on the other side of the Abyss, it turns out that even the ego can be welcomed back as a coherent part of the awakened whole without any issues.

The way I am describing my experience here suggests a single, magnificent coherence event that reveals the alignment behind everything all at once, accompanied by a lot of imaginal fireworks and the peals of angel's trumpets. As you've no doubt realized by now, I am prone to these kinds of dramatic mystical experiences, and this event was no exception. But, that's just one way of experiencing it. For other people, coherence on the other side of the Abyss may be more of a gradual process, a whole chain of happenings taking place over many years or even decades, where different aspects are gradually brought into coherence.

To illustrate, here's a story from Jack, comparing his ongoing process of coherence to my sudden definitive moment:

> I think we've gone through a similar process at a different speed. For you it was instant, and for me it's been over several years. I have felt greater and greater coherence with all the different levels of life, like I am unifying with them. There are lots of stories not just one.
>
> The overall theme is a deep trust in life, and a realization that I am life, and a letting go into all of that. It's like a surrender. I don't have to do anything to become more free, because the ego doesn't have to control anything. So, I just allow myself as life to take my form, and I use my form as it needs to be used. You could say that this is my sole mission, but I don't have to do anything to achieve it.
>
> I used to be dragged kicking and screaming into things, but now my trust in life is so much higher. I'll know when I'm supposed to do something, or where I'm supposed to go, and I just do it. There's a lot less inner resistance and I don't feel like I need to know as much as I used to. So I can trust in the flow of life.

Your own final coherence might come as a spectacular divine revelation or as a quiet whisper of relief after a long series of insights. Either way, there will come a moment when the perfection of the whole finally snaps into place. When that happens, there will be no doubt in your mind that the work of Descent has been completed. It's like a veil suddenly lifts, or like dawn suddenly breaks. For perhaps the first time in a long time, you suddenly feel human again. You realize that your work of being alchemized in the Below is finished. It is time to begin the Return.

Bringing home the elixir

In awakening the Above, we become purified of delusions, constructs, and flawed conditioning. In the crucible of the Below, on the other hand, our shortcomings are not shed; they are forged into diamonds. Coherence makes it clear that the totality of your being *is* the elixir. Your traumas, troubles, fears, pains, and wounds *are* the elixirs. Your body and its history—biographical, intergenerational, and karmic—*are* the elixirs. Every aspect of your entire being, without exception, are integral, necessary parts of this sacred, blessed whole.

Of course, your equanimity, nondual realizations, open-heartedness, divinity, and other Above qualities are all elixirs too. Elixirs flow both from Above and Below in equal measure. Unlike the elixirs from the Above, however, the elixirs you find in the Below can be deeply unsettling to ego-selves. They will not match the fantasies that egos have about what spirituality is all about. So-called spiritual people will reject these elixirs, and it's very possible your community and loved ones might as well—just like you yourself always used to do in the past. But, just like during the rest of your transit through the Below, you'll now have no choice but to surrender to what's happening. Once the Return begins, you simply must find a way to bring these elixirs back home to the Middle, even if you become hated or persecuted for it. Even at the expense of your life (just ask Jesus, who was killed for sharing his!).

Listen to Jack describe how his childhood traumas turned into elixirs, and how this result differed from his Above-influenced expectations:

> When I came into spiritual awakening, I thought the goal was up and out: escape. I ascend out of all of my problems and that's it; I'm done. I was running away from my darkness. But what has happened more and more over time is that I've stopped seeing the darkness as the opposite of light. And I've entered into it and embraced it without any need to change it.
>
> There's nothing wrong with it. There's no right or wrong here; the darkness simply is what it is. It's rich, and it's beautiful, and it's interesting, and it's to be met with dignity. The darkness deserves dignity, and you're not giving it that dignity when you're telling it that it should be something else.
>
> From this perspective, it seems like these traumas I carry are almost like these nodes of wisdom. They're parts of the goddess that are waiting to be found, and once found and met and tenderly embraced, they contain the wisdom and the compassion of the goddess. Her wisdom and compassion flows through them.
>
> Each of these nodes is part of a network of traumas that exist inside the earth and inside our bodies, not only as individuals but within our collective body as humanity. By meeting this trauma, it causes a ripple effect, a chain reaction of healing that moves throughout the whole system.

Having learned how his traumas are actually his gifts, Jack now meets with clients through workshops, private sessions, YouTubes, and podcasts, helping them to heal and liberate their own "nodes of wisdom." In order to do that, Jack had to create what Plotkin calls a "delivery vehicle for his soul's gifts," a mechanism for bringing the elixirs he has discovered within the depths of the Below out into the Middle. To make that happen, he needed to walk away from a career in medical research in order to establish a full-time teaching and healing practice called My Rising Rose Sanctuary of Divine Healing (www.myrisingrose.com).

In my own case, the book you are reading right is one of my elixirs, forged in the Below, that I must deliver. I decided to write it under the name Oholomo, "the Light Bearer," a title that was whispered to me in the middle of the night when I was in the throes of the Descent. The point of using this pen name is to deflect attention away from me personally, while still being able to release this elixir out into the world so that it may be helpful to others. My gift is not to be a spiritual teacher or guide, but rather a map-maker of the territory. I like to say that I'm like the ticket seller who hands you a map of the cave-system as you enter the gate, while Jack is like the tourguide who walks you through the caves himself. We each have our roles to play, and in time, you will find yours as well.

CHAPTER FOUR

Navigating the darkness

Having surveyed the layers of the Below in the previous chapter, let's introduce some practical advice on navigating this territory. This chapter intentionally provides more of a macro-level overview of a wide range of practices, rather than a step-by-step guide to any specific techniques. Moreover, while trying to be as broad as possible, the discussion here is by no means comprehensive. For these reasons, I want to again recommend some of the books listed at the end of Chapter Two. Many of those titles have step-by-step descriptions that fill in the details and complement the discussion here.

Safety first

I like the concept of "spiritual sovereignty," which I got from my friend Misha, who got it from the spiritual teacher Adyashanti. This means that no one else can decide what spiritual path is right for you, but also implies that you must accept the consequences of your own choices. The bottom line is that if you decide to engage the Below using practices such as the ones I identify in this chapter, you must accept that there are dangers and take full responsibility for what happens.

Navigating the Below is a high-risk activity, and there are no guarantees of safety. This process will demand that you fully surrender to your worst fears—to madness and even to death itself. You may feel like most of the time you're walking blindfolded on a tightrope over a chasm without a net. During the Descent, you will be working out a huge load of your past karma, traumas, and complexes. This is messy work that will give rise to mental agitation, emotional turbulence, and general instability.

One important way to attend to your safety and well-being is to reach out for help and support when you need it. That support might take any number of forms. It might be a knowledgeable teacher or guide who you meet with on a regular basis. It might be connecting on an ad hoc basis with someone who seems like they might have something helpful to say about what you are going through right at the moment. It might be a group of like-minded spiritual travelers who are going through the Descent together.

Whatever form of support is most helpful and feels nurturing is probably right for you. If you ask me, though, you should seek out people who are deeply familiar with the kinds of experiences we're talking about in this book. It makes no sense if you need help with your motorcycle to call a plumber. Likewise, it makes no sense if you need help with the Below to seek advice from an Above-based priest, monastic, or spiritual teacher. At best, their advice could be off-base; at worst, quite harmful. Another thing I would suggest is to seek out a range of different guides or supporters. Since experiences of the Below are so variable from person to person, it is often beneficial to hear from a wide range of opinions and perspectives.

Even while I am encouraging you to establish a network of support that works for you, it is crucial to guard against over-reliance on other people. Always remember that any kind of supporter who undermines your autonomy, integrity, or freedom as an individual agent—even if unintentionally—is counterproductive. Any kind of supporter who makes you feel unworthy or ashamed—even if unintentionally—is potentially damaging your process. It is equally harmful to place a supporter or guide on a pedestal, to see them as infallible, or to become infatuated with them. Don't give away your power, energy, autonomy, or wholeness to others under any circumstances. Doing so may completely derail your process.

Another important safety concern is the need to ground yourself. Being familiar with grounding practices is a critical skill. It means that you have a tool at your disposal whereby you can soothe your system physically, mentally, and energetically. If yours is an authentic Descent into the Below, you will undoubtedly encounter moments in your journey where things get extremely difficult, out of control, or completely terrifying. When those moments come, it will be too late to start learning to ground yourself then. You will find it far easier if you already have several grounding practices that you have been doing daily all along. That being said, if you're already traversing the Below, your only choice may be to develop or strengthen your grounding practices as soon as possible.

Grounding means your mind relaxes, your energy level settles down, and your body sensations connect with gravity and the earth. Common grounding exercises include qigong, martial arts, yoga, breathwork, visualization, and many other traditional spiritual practices. Physical exercise—ranging from going for a gentle walk to heart-pounding interval training—is nearly always grounding. A Kundalini teacher I know advocates gardening, making pottery, and eating meat and heavier foods. Other people I know are into playing music, creating art, masturbation, salt baths, making physical contact with the earth, or lying down on it and visualizing themselves melting into the ground. Whatever works for you that down-regulates your system and gets you back into your body (particularly the lower portion of it) is grounding for you.

As you become adjusted to the Descent, you'll find that you can "turn up and down the volume," so to speak, on the intensity of your experiences. All the other practices I outline in this chapter help you to enhance your connection with the Below, but grounding is what smooths the ride. If things start moving too quickly, you can slow them down a bit by increasing the percentage of grounding you are doing. If it still feels like it's too much, you can switch to doing 100 percent grounding for a while.

Here's a story from Misha about how a grounding practice helped her to turn the volume down on an overwhelming spiritual experience that arose at an inopportune time:

> A few months ago, I was coming back over the mountains having done a retreat. There was inclement weather, and I was going up into elevation on a twisty road that had pretty steep drop-offs. It was probably not a good idea to drive with such low visibility and a slick highway!

As I drove, I had to stop a couple times because there was something going on inside of me. It looked like I was driving up into a cloud. Everything was so magical, so divinely beautiful. I don't think it could have been more awesome. I felt this pressure building in my heart area, which turned out to be Christ energy expanding. Eventually, I pulled over and spent maybe forty-five minutes there in my car, twitching and moaning, and like, you know, being Christ.

Eventually, it calmed down enough that I could get back on the road. And so I'm driving carefully and slowly and really glad there's no one coming behind me tailgating or whatever. Then when I was maybe twenty or thirty minutes away from the first town, and I just had a cringing feeling like, "I just can't go there." It was almost like I can't be in that energy of civilization.

Earlier I had passed this place where there were signs for a nature area or campground or something. And I was like, "Let me go back and pull off there." As I'm on a narrow mountain pass, I'm literally driving in the middle of the road because the drop-off is too close to where my lane is. And the snow is coming down, sticking on the road. By this time, I'm not in the Christ experience anymore, I'm in the God experience. Everything is magnificent, you know, the snow, the air, the mountains, the drop-off, everything. When I reached a safe enough place, I parked my vehicle and just let that experience overtake me for another forty-five minutes or so.

Finally, I'm like, "Okay, I only have so much gas in the vehicle. And I'm really not good to be alone in a car that I'm not sure I can keep warm when it's snowing. And it's going to get colder tonight, so there is an actual real danger of freezing."

Fortunately, there was cell service. So I called my Tibetan Buddhist temple, the local place. And I get their office manager administrative person. Now, a qualification for that position is that they have to be devoted to the rinpoche's teachings and be skilled with all kinds of states, because she's the point of contact when there's in-person retreats, and people are going to be going through all kinds of stuff.

So I told her, "I'm having some kind of awakening experience, very blissful, but still, I'm not able to be functional, to do what I need to do. I'm in the mountains, it's snowing, I need to get myself home." And so what she suggested I do was to breathe in and out of the hara. And she asked, "Do you have a chant?" I said, "White Tara always works for me." And she's like, "Great, do that."

So that's what I did, and I was able to get home in one shot. I practiced this intensive grounding continuously for like another fifty or sixty minutes while driving. And I didn't get hijacked either by bliss or by cringing. It kept me present and focused and grounded in my body and in ordinary reality. I wasn't overtaken either by the blissful God experience or being unable to navigate through the places that energetically felt yucky. It gave me some space from the awakening process that was happening, which I needed because I wasn't in a setting where it was safe to just surrender to that completely.

To me, Misha's drive home from the retreat is a good metaphor for the whole journey through the Below. You're headed off into the unknown along a treacherous mountain road with steep drop-offs. There will be tremendous ups and downs, intensely blissful and unpleasant experiences at every turn. You'll probably find yourself to be overwhelmed, and even incapacitated at times. There's a real chance you won't make it back home in one piece unless you can ground yourself when you need to.

In Misha's case, she was lucky to have cell service and the presence of mind to call for help when she needed it. But what if her phone didn't work? It would have been safer if she already had that grounding practice in her toolbox, part of her regular repertoire of practices, wouldn't you agree?

Facing challenging experiences

The Descent into the Below is a descent into the unconscious portions of the psyche. Or rather, it's an explosion of the unconscious portions of the psyche out into consciousness. It's as if Pandora's Box were to be opened and all the hidden contents of the mind—the sublime, the beautiful, the shadows, and the nightmares—all were to come flooding out. Among these contents, be prepared for difficult memories and traumas of all kinds to emerge. Some of these traumas will be expected. If you were entirely honest with yourself, you'd have known they were hidden away in there all along. Others will take you completely by surprise—memories that were completely repressed, or that you thought you had already worked through. The point is that every last vestige of unconscious pain simply must be reckoned with.

When challenges arise in the process of Descent, there are two different approaches one may take, which I refer to as the masculine and the feminine. (I know that these binary gendered terms are going to be off-putting for some people. If they are bothersome to you, please just replace them as you read with yang and yin, or any other terms you like. In my case, as a cisgendered heterosexual male who is deeply in love with a whole retinue of goddesses and other feminine spirit guides, it feels natural and important to refer to this approach in feminine terms.)

What I call the masculine approach represents the typical advice given in Buddhist and Advaita circles (Above-based traditions not coincidentally dominated by male spiritual heroes and teachers). This is to hold difficult experiences in one's awareness until they dissolve or resolve. In the Theravada Buddhist meditation retreats where I spent much of my twenties, the instructions were phrased more or less as follows: "These afflictions are simply unpleasant body sensations; they are impermanent. Observe them with equanimity and they will pass away." Advaita teachers I have heard, on the other hand, have tended to give an instruction like "See yourself as the awareness that contains all experiences." Christian teachings might have you similarly rest your mind in God or silence.

These kinds of approaches are paradigmatic of Above-style spirituality: by holding the mind steady in a state of higher consciousness, all Maras can be vanquished. One's mind is purified of these "defilements," as they put it in Buddhism, or purified of "sin" as the Christians say.

In contrast, the feminine approach is for difficult memories, traumas, and other challenges to be seen, recognized, and eventually even welcomed into the wholeness of your being. In order to start to do this, you must surrender to them, sink down into them, and deeply feel them. On the surface, it may look like the practitioner is doing the same thing as in the masculine approach: sitting with the experience and waiting. However, the attitude is completely different. Rather than objectifying the negative experience, disidentifying from it, reframing it, staying aloof from it, or observing it dispassionately, the feminine approach is to fully invite it in without any resistance and allow it to totally eviscerate you.

Think back to the two versions of the Buddha myth with which I started this book. In the traditional story, the Buddha is the archetypal masculine spiritual hero. He is strong, resolute, equanimous, determined, unshakable, and in control. In my recasting of the story, however, I replaced these attributes with their feminine counterparts. I made the Buddha vulnerable, emotional, relational, and surrendering. I made that change for this book because, while masculine approaches to spirituality can be quite effective in the Above, I have learned that the best way to relate to the Below is to totally and utterly embrace the feminine.

To illustrate how this principle applies in real life, let me tell you a story about something that happened to me when I was somewhat early in my own journey into the Below. One of my kids was having a surgery to correct a congenital condition. It was not a life-threatening situation, but it was a major procedure. Although up to that point in my awakening process I had been very comfortably ensconced in the Above, with a high degree of equanimity and very little emotion arising other than tranquility, I noticed that I was feeling some trepidation about her safety and well-being when undergoing such a procedure. As she was wheeled into the operating room to go under the knife, I closed my eyes and tuned in to my body sensations. A tremendous amount of anxiety suddenly welled up in the form of sharp little waves of sensation fluttering about in my body. These sensations were surprisingly uncomfortable, and I noticed an impulse to recoil away from them.

Now, my years of mindfulness training had prepared me for precisely this moment. I knew that the "proper" thing to do with this kind of feeling (or, as we dismissively called it in my Buddhist circles, "attachment") was to dispassionately and analytically dissect the sensations that were appearing. To observe where they began and where they finished, their temperature, the speed of their oscillation, how they changed over time, and other details. I knew the teaching was to neutrally note these qualities as they were arising, seeing that all of it was an impermanent cloud of impersonal, transitory phenomena. I had done that many times in the past, and that's what I "should" have done now.

But, as I sat there, something led me to just surrender instead of trying to observe, and to let the sensations completely take over my being. Among the sharp and prickly feelings of anxiety and the impulse to recoil, I now also felt my displeasure at the whole experience, my frustration with having to feel these sensations, and a tension in my chest that felt like sadness or like I wanted to cry. All of this swelled and churned like waves in the ocean during a storm. I felt gutted, like I was completely falling apart.

This went on for a while—perhaps twenty or thirty minutes—and somehow I just sat there surrendering to what was happening and sinking down into all of it. After a time, though, I noticed the sensations changing. The sharpness and prickliness seemed to give way to something more gentle. Just then, in a surprisingly sudden shift, it was like the ocean of sensation that was so uncomfortable in my chest area suddenly dissolved into a warm glow. It was precisely the feeling that I remembered from when my daughter was a toddler years ago, and I used to pick her up and hold her to my chest to comfort her when she was crying. I could feel her little warm body pressed against mine, and at the same time, a kind of outward extension of bittersweet tenderness from my heart area.

Feeling like I was actually holding her in my arms right at that moment, I sensed a deep connection with her, like I was somehow sharing the trauma her unconscious body was undergoing in the operating room. I understood then that the anxiety I had felt earlier—while it may have felt cold, sharp, and unpleasant—was really just a form of love in disguise. I also understood that my vulnerability to be able to suffer so deeply out of love for my child was not a problem—it was actually one of the most beautiful and important parts of my humanness. Pain, suffering, and vulnerability can be welcomed as part of the whole.

Do you recognize the similarities between the story I just told and my revised version of the Buddha myth in the preface? That shift from masculine to feminine is precisely the way to access the elixirs of the Below, no matter which Mara we are facing. I could never have discovered these elixirs if I had approached my experience using the techniques my mindfulness training had taught me. If I had exercised a detached posture toward my experience of anxiety, I could certainly have strengthened my equanimity, my appreciation of impermanence, and my resolve in the face of suffering. However, by surrendering to the anxiety instead, I found the blessings of vulnerability, connection, love, and tenderness lying at the core of an unpleasant yet entirely human experience. Different approaches, different elixirs.

The realization I had on that day was highly impactful for me, and from that point onwards, I applied that same feminine response to all of my weird and difficult experiences as I Descended further and further into the Below. Rather than observing these experiences with Above-based techniques, I relaxed, let go, and let them into my being. Sooner or later (sometimes much later!), I always got similar results. Some of these experiences took longer than others to sit with and fully digest; a few I had to come back to again and again for months or even years. But if there ever were any challenges or difficulties in my process of Descent, it was always only because I hadn't yet managed to fully surrender.

Now, the advice I would have been given by my Above-based teachers about all of those experiences would have been that they are just clusters of impermanent phenomena, which I should equanimously observe and allow to pass away. Such things are distractions or delusions, they would have said; don't get involved. If you have a lot of training in the techniques of Above-based spirituality, your ego will probably try to establish a sense of normalcy by falling back on that kind of advice. However, if you are encountering difficulties in the process of Descent, retreating into the aloofness and equanimity of Above is simply not going to work for you in the long run.

That being said, you won't be able to retreat into the Middle either. Don't cling to the tools of conventional psychology, biology, neuroscience, or other knowledge systems of the Middle to try to explain the Below in a linear way. Undoubtedly, again, your ego will attempt to do this in order to tell itself that everything is okay. But, don't allow your mind to settle on straightforward explanations or fixed notions of reality. When the ego struggles to explain what's happening, just drop the effort to understand and surrender to fully feeling the experience instead. Sink down into experiencing whatever is going on, up close and intimately, in all of its gory detail.

Suspending your attempts to explain or understand, as well as your familiar tools and techniques, will likely make you feel naked, alone, vulnerable, or terrified. Surrender to those feelings as well, feeling them fully as they arise. If you need help with surrendering, try a surrender prayer or mantra. I wrote this one spontaneously one day, and used it daily for many months as I circled around the Abyss:

> *Divine Mother,*
> *I surrender to your grace.*
> *Embrace me, keep me safe, teach me.*
> *I am yours.*

I found that these words helped ease my mind. One of the reasons I think this mantra worked well for me is that it set up a situation I call "surrender by proxy." For me, the Descent was at many points so harrowing that it seemed impossible for me to surrender to it directly. Instead, I decided to place my trust and faith in the hands of the divine mother in all of her forms (María, Kuan Yin, Sol, Bachué, and all the rest). Whereas I could not manage to surrender myself to the Abyss, I found that I could surrender totally to her, trusting that she would guide and protect me. Of course, as I mentioned in the Abyss section of the previous chapter, you eventually have to let go of all crutches and pass through the birth canal naked and alone. But, I found that surrender by proxy eased my approach and gave me more confidence as I came near.

While I will present a lot of other practices in this chapter, I would say that, ultimately, the only thing you need to do to successfully navigate the challenges of the Below is simply to adopt this attitude of surrender. If you're encountering the effects of trauma lurking in your body or your energy system is ravaged and battered, surrender to feeling it. If you see visions of dark threatening entities or find yourself in the underworld being torn into pieces, surrender to the experience. Faced with existential terror, madness, or the fear of annihilation, surrender to all of it, without exception. Once you fully surrender to the Below, it will reveal its gifts.

(That being the case, remember what I said above about grounding, specifically how it can provide a counterbalance to surrender. Learning how to pendulate between the acceleration of surrender and the self-care of grounding is a crucial skill that will ensure your safety throughout the Descent.)

Meditation and other psychedelics

The chief way that we can court the Descent, invite the Below to become more manifest in our lives, deepen our experience of it, and eventually discover its elixirs, is to break down the protective wall built by the ego-self in an attempt to keep us safe. I imagine that most readers of this book have already entered into an awakening process of some kind or another, or at least have tasted enough to know that those walls the ego perpetually keeps us ensconced in can at times be lowered. Sometimes this happens spontaneously, sometimes intentionally; sometimes it's over in a flash, sometimes it lasts for a long time.

However it happens, the lowering of the ego's reality-walls opens up an infinite number of possibilities for how reality is experienced or how it manifests. You might already be quite familiar with practices that can reliably drop the wall and allow you to experience the Above—perhaps techniques that elicit awareness, spaciousness, emptiness, bliss, tranquility, or something similar. One of the most significant lessons in one's Descent is discovering what kinds of tools or practices allow the Below to manifest.

I like to refer to all such ego-wall-lowering techniques as psychedelic. Etymologically speaking, this word includes the Greek for "mind" or "soul" (*psyche*) and for "visible" or "manifest" (*dêlos*). So, to me, a psychedelic could be anything that makes the deeper aspects of the psyche visible or manifest. Everyone will, of course, think of psychedelic drugs first. Personally, I have only done psychedelic drugs a few times—in college and for recreational purposes—and I quickly decided that it wasn't for me. But, my studies of the use of hallucinogenics among shamanic cultures and conversations with some psychonaut friends has led me to have an appreciation for how powerfully these substances can knock down that reality-wall and evoke profoundly imaginal experiences.

However, while psychedelic drugs can reliably breach the ego's defenses, I would strongly urge caution because these drugs are potentially unreliable in what kind of experience they plunge you into on the other side of that wall. As a beginner using such drugs, there's often no telling what will happen. You might be thrust into an experience of the Above or the Below, you might experience extreme bliss or terror, you might experience sublime spiritual states or hellish nightmares. Drug-induced psychedelic states can potentially be therapeutic, but they can also cause irreparable psychological trauma to the journeyer.

Thankfully, with the clinical usage of these compounds in therapeutic environments, we have found that the nature and intensity of psychedelic experiences can be much better controlled with careful attention to "set and setting." Even so, in speaking with friends who engage regularly with psilocybin, ayahuasca, 5-MeO-DMT, MDMA, LSD and related substances to periodically propel themselves beyond the reality-wall for purposes of spiritual growth, they invariably tell me that their psychedelic sessions are unpredictable and that they need to do a ton of other practices in between sessions in order to integrate their experiences.

If after careful considerations of the risks you decide to use psychedelic drugs to enhance your experience of the Below, then that's your own choice. Remember the principle of spiritual sovereignty.

Fortunately, however, there are plenty of psychedelic practices (to use the more expansive definition of the term) that don't involve drugs of any kind. Many of these practices are long-established parts of certain religious, spiritual, and cultural traditions, and many of them are already well known in contemporary Western spiritual circles.

On the more intensive end of the spectrum are practices that normally take place within retreat settings, including fasting, vision quests, meditation retreats, long-term sensory deprivation (e.g., so-called "dark retreats"), and so forth. Such intensive experiences can produce visions, revelations, and mystical experiences that are every bit as powerful as any drug. These also have the same downsides of being potentially unpredictable and overwhelming. Again, if you decide to engage in intensive practice in retreat settings, do so with discretion, under skillful supervision, and paying close attention to grounding and integration.

However, there are also many highly psychoactive techniques that can be practiced more regularly as part of your daily routine, which means that, on the whole, they will be more easily integrated. I'm thinking here of all sorts of different meditations, breathwork, mantras, yoga, qigong, visualization, prayer, active imagination, automatic writing, dream journaling, lucid dreaming, shamanic journeying, drumming, dance, ecstatic movement, and other trance-inducing techniques. When practiced in high daily doses, these can be every bit as psychedelic as drugs or retreats, and your experiences can also be just as powerful. When practiced in more moderate dosages, these can be safer and easier to integrate than the more intensive options. If your daily dosage drops even lower, these practices may become inert, devoid of any kind of psychedelic power at all. In my view, this flexibility is a great advantage. Particularly when combined with grounding practices, this gives you some power to control the intensity of the experiences you are cultivating.

During my three-year awakening the Below process (which, again, should not be thought of as normative), I figured out which practices worked for me personally and administered them at the maximum dose that I could handle in order to maintain a high psychedelic intensity. In general, I practiced about four and a half to five hours per day of a blend of seated meditation, walking meditation, yoga, qigong, and drumming-assisted visualization. This schedule allowed me to immerse myself in the Below while also maintaining healthy integration with the everyday life of family, work, and other obligations. I continually tweaked the blend of practices as my experiences shifted, and occasionally backed off when I wanted to more carefully navigate difficult territory.

What works for you, no doubt, will be different than what worked for me. My main advice is to always prioritize integration and balance. If you're ever feeling like things are unsafe or unsustainable, back off and increase your practice of grounding. In a pinch, it is always a good idea to take a break from all psychedelic practices, and to prioritize grounding until you get your footing back.

Opening the sensory channels

Whatever psychedelic practices you are using, if you wish to enhance and deepen your experiences of the Below, my advice is to work on opening up as many of your sensory channels to it as you can. For whatever reason, different people seem to have natural aptitudes for engaging with certain kinds of sensory stimuli while others remain relatively underdeveloped. In my case, my sense of vision and body sensations were naturally my strongest channels. For me, that meant that the whole range of imaginal experiences, energy flows, spirit visitations, and other aspects of the Below manifested most clearly as visionary and tactile experiences.

My visions began spontaneously. As I lay in bed before sleep one night, I started to have what I can only describe as a dream-like experience while I was still awake. The imagery was extremely vivid: I saw my body surrounded by an energetic egg of white light, which in turn was lying in the coils of a black snake. I could see the eyes of the snake, and the details of the coils quite clearly with eyes closed, although it would disappear if I opened my eyelids. From this initial event, I went on to have a great number of vividly real and profoundly meaningful visions—several per day—throughout the rest of my sojourn in the Below.

Almost all of these visions were accompanied by body sensations. These could be subtle, such as a general feeling of warmth or safety, or quite strong, such as a rush of fear or sexual energy. Over time, I realized that certain configurations of body sensations were associated with certain spirits, guides, or other imaginal entities I was seeing in my visions. For example, there was the spirit of an old Indigenous South American woman that appeared to me visually, always accompanied by a feeling of weight on my back like I was carrying a backpack. There was the black jaguar spirit that felt like a rush of fear up the left back side of my body, which sprang out in front of me from my left shoulder. There was a blonde angelic feminine figure whose presence I could feel walking alongside my right side, and whose hair sometimes would glance my cheek.

What I didn't experience with any clarity was auditory signals. Only twice did I hear a voice clearly saying something to me. But other people are different, reporting frequent auditory communications in words or celestial music or other sounds. Here is how Jack, for example, talks about his interactions with his guides:

> In terms of connecting with guides or spiritual beings, it started when I was asking myself questions, and I noticed that my head was either nodding or shaking in response to those questions. And then I realized that my body was being used by higher beings to answer the questions of my mind. I asked, "Are these my guides?" And then my head starts nodding. My mind was blown.
>
> And then I asked a question, "What is the purpose of my life?" And the answer came through. I would say it was the auditory sense, but I wouldn't even describe it as words. It was a felt sense, which could be interpreted into words. And the words were "You are to be a teacher and leader of man. You're here to save humanity." And it came from this place of utter peace, and truth and sincerity. There was no hint of ego or anything; it was just pure.
>
> As time went on, I developed these auditory connections with spiritual beings where I would hear their voice inside my mind. You know, people talk about their mind's eye; it was like my mind's ear. Sometimes they'll send me images, or I'll close my eyes. And it's like I'm watching a movie; I'll just be experiencing all this stuff. And they'll just explain things to me through that.
>
> And on rare occasions, maybe only two or three times, I've heard an actual auditory sound in the room. And every time it's the Morrigan. And there'll be her talking to me, you know, I'll hear her saying my name in the room.
>
> But it's mostly a feeling sense that could be interpreted into words. And that's a fascinating form of communication. It's almost like it's ten times the speed of speaking. So it's like these waves of energy moving back and forth. And so you can have these massive

resolutions and insights and all sorts of stuff, in a super short period of time.

The main advice I want to share here is to start with the sensory channels that naturally seem to be the most open, and take steps to enhance those. If you naturally start to see visions, then perhaps you should move your practice time into a darkened environment where you can more readily see them. (I moved my morning practice from the back deck to my dark basement for exactly this reason.) If you naturally are prone to bodily sensations, then perhaps do some kind of practice that will enhance your receptivity to them. (For me, I discovered that repetitive movement practice such as qigong or ecstatic dancing was most effective.) If you are receiving auditory messages, then maybe you need to work more with sound. (That may perhaps mean moving to a totally silent practice space, or chanting out loud, or singing bowls, or some other kind of sound-based practice.)

Once you have figured out how to maximize the channels that come to you naturally, you can then turn to developing the ones that don't. There isn't a one-size-fits-all answer to how to enhance sensory channels. For me, I found that I could enhance my auditory channel by ringing a bell and listening to shamanic drumming as part of my daily practice. I also found that the smell of burning tobacco, perfume, and other aromatic offerings had an evocative sensory effect. I am not telling you what to do specifically, but rather suggesting that you closely pay attention to how the practices you are engaged in affect the sensory channels, and see if you can find a combination of set, setting, and technique that enhances the clarity and quality of the messages you are receiving. Whatever the specific details, the goal is to create imaginal experiences that you tangibly see, feel, hear, smell, and taste. Immersive multi-sensory experiences that are manifesting across as many sensory dimensions as you can manage will have a notable effect on strengthening and deepening your experience of the Below.

Over time you'll create strong associations between certain sensory cues and certain experiences of the Below. Here's Misha talking about the benefits of a multisensory immersive practice:

> My primary, low hanging fruit sense modes are tactile—which is the whole body, not just surface—and I tend to get a lot of visuals.

And then there's felt sense stuff, which I'm not sure if that's exactly just body or energy or what. Into that, I have introduced scent. I have medicine objects like specific stones, little bear fetishes, a twig from my ash tree outside. Of course, there is music, instrumentals, songs, and chants. On the more tactile end, a teddy bear that's soft, so my system is like, "Ohhh ... soothing ... soft ..." and that's combined with my image of Bear as protector. And then darkness and posture.

And, if I'm wanting to enrich things, I also pay attention to multi-modality: using thoughts, emotions, bodily sensations, desires, and actions. The more immersive my experiences, the more richness. When processes show up spontaneously at a low level of intensity, it can be much easier for me to just disregard them and not actively engage. However, more active engagement enriches the experiences. And the more full and intense they are, and the more any particular element is repeatedly included, then there's this wonderful byproduct or associated effect of cueing the nervous system to a pay attention to that kind of information in the future. Even if there's not conscious attention being paid, the nervous system is paying attention to things in the environment.

The more you enrich it and the longer it lasts, the more it installs, the more deeply the system is sinking into the experience. The nervous system learns this, and then these specific sensory elements can later act as cues to prep the system to say, "I'm going into this state, or I'm doing this kind of work, or I'm going to engage in whatever."

Protectors, guides, and higher powers

I was lucky that, when my Descent began, I was almost immediately introduced to Bachué. Thus, my journey into the Below began with a positive and empowering encounter. The fact that I was having such a vivid vision of this goddess was bizarre, and her half-demonic appearance was disconcerting to be sure. But, I had no doubt that the content of my visions was beneficent and supportive, and that allowed me to more easily accept and embrace what was happening.

My friend Lisa also experienced a spontaneous encounter with the beneficent and helpful masculine presences of God and Jesus right at the beginning of her process:

> I think that my whole life I felt very misunderstood. That's been a big theme for me. Once, I felt like everyone was watching me

and laughing at me, and I was feeling so horribly embarrassed. I lay in my bed and I was just feeling really small, and all of a sudden, it was just immediate that God and Jesus were here. It was a knowing with my whole experience, an emotional knowing where everything just clicked in. I knew it was them, and I knew that we were all merged. Everything couldn't be more perfect, you know, just amazing.

I felt it physically that there was this masculine energy just coming behind me and holding me, supporting me, comforting me, and offering me this soothing newness when I felt so alone. It felt completely real. Actually, it kind of scared me a little bit because it literally felt like a physical person by me, like actual physical touch.

I was never raised religious or anything like that, but I feel that energy all the time now. And I feel them a lot when I walk, like somebody next to me. Towards the end, Jesus has been coming in and teaching me different things. And then, recently, he told me to see all men as him. And, he's been giving me like hints and clues about how to open myself more or how to go deeper into the awakening. It's been a communication for myself only, just the opening of energetic space. It's passive, but it's also active. It's a total allowance, opening and just allowing. That's how I kind of describe it.

Other people are not so fortunate as Lisa and I, and may spend time struggling alone in the Below without any helpful beings who can provide guidance. For this reason, I think that finding a beneficial higher power is a top priority. The Below is a dark and fearsome place, but a powerful and compassionate being can hold your hand and light the way as you traverse the underworld.

If you don't currently have a guide, who can you call upon to be one? There is no one right answer, no single highest being that is a good fit for everyone's unique imaginal configuration. The right answer is to reach out to whoever will work for you. If you're unsure, one exercise I sometimes suggest people do is what I call the "crashing plane thought experiment." Imagine or visualize that you are flying in a plane when suddenly both engines fail. You start plummeting to the ground, and there is no chance of survival. If this were to actually happen to you, in that minute or so that you have left to live before the plane meets its fiery end, who would your desperate heart spontaneously call out to for help? Who might possibly have the power to perform a miracle? Who would you wish to hold your hand as you die?

If there's someone who comes to mind while doing this thought experiment, then try calling out to that being for help in the Below. If it's not a particular entity, but an abstract quality such as Truth, Love, or Compassion, then go ahead and use that. However, if nothing in particular comes to mind, then you can also just make a general call. In one of your practice sessions, when you have built up some psychedelic momentum and your sensory channels feel particularly open, try asking for a higher power to make themselves available to you.

Who will hear your call and emerge as your helper(s) may not be possible to guess beforehand. Remember the story I told about how I automatically assumed that my guides would be Asian deities, and how I initially rejected outright the idea of working with María? Since that time, I have also developed a close relationship with the Buddhist goddess of mercy, Kuan Yin. But I also am very intimate with the radiant Pagan sun goddess Sol, who I had never even heard of before she appeared to me. A whole panoply of other guides, including angelic feminine goddess figures as well as power animals, have all become a regular part of my imaginal world, but I would never have guessed that they would play such a central role. Remember also Jack's story about initially misunderstanding Kali's intentions to nourish him due to her frightful appearance. My point is simply that help may come in the form you least expect, so don't reject whatever guidance comes to you just because it doesn't fit with your expectations.

That being said, you don't want to just jump into a relationship with a powerful being willy nilly. My suggestion is to make the call for a higher power and see who shows up. When they do, if they are a being of light that is universally recognized as beneficial—a Buddha or bodhisattva, Jesus, Virgin Mary, a Hindu deity, Ramana Maharshi, etc.—then you can trust them.

But, what if the being who answers your call is not one you recognize? In this case, I would advise that you spend some time asking them questions. Who are they? What kinds of energy do they embody? What kinds of values do they stand for? Is there another being standing behind them that is even more powerful? If so, what are their qualities? Also an important question to ask any being is, will you be able to "break up" with them if things don't work out? (The answer better be yes—no truly beneficial being will require vows of fidelity or other kinds of obligations.)

Take a few days and do some research, or return to ask them more questions and get an increasingly better feel for who this being is. Only when you've fully vetted them and feel very confident should you let them into your life and let them advise you on your journey. And, once you do, remember you are spiritually sovereign and don't ever let anyone—no matter who they are—force you into something that isn't right for you. Your relationship with a higher power guide or protector should always feel beneficial, supportive, and empowering. You should never feel like you have taken on the inferior role in an asymmetrical relationship, or like you have lost any of your autonomy. A true guide or protector strengthens and nourishes your boundaries and personal power, never depletes or diminishes them.

As you dwell in the Below, you will continue to meet more and more beneficial beings who can serve different types of functions in your journey. Some of these will be more powerful than others. In my case, María, Kuan Yin, and Sol are at the apex. For me, they are all actually manifestations of different facets of the Mother, by which I mean the absolute highest, most sacred, and holy source of love in the cosmos. In addition to them, various ancestral and animal spirits provide specific types of assistance. The jaguar helps with journeys into the underworld; the owl with death and ghosts; one ancestral guide with absorbing troubles and generating blessings; another with enhancing my perception of the imaginal; and many others. Each one of these beings has their own particular potencies, and are called forth to meet particular circumstances. Bachué, my body deva, is the overall container or embodiment for all of these beneficial powers, the vehicle by which their blessings come out into the world. Of course, your pantheon and how you see them fitting together will be totally different than mine. As it should be. Since no two of us are exactly the same, no two imaginal worlds will line up perfectly eye-to-eye!

Once you've worked with your guides for a while and have developed deeper trust in them, it may be symbolically and emotionally significant to make a commitment to them in some way. Here's Jack's story of how he got a tattoo as an act of commitment to his dragon guides:

> This tattoo was kind of like a blessing and imbuing of the quality of the Dragon into me, into my skin. It was like a sign of my commitment to the dragons.

I'll often channel them and they'll say things to me like, "Our greatest obstacle in supporting you is you. You know, it's humans resisting us and preventing us from being able to support them because humans subconsciously believe that they have to do everything by themselves, and don't realize that they're part of this cosmos, which is a single living being. We can do a lot of the work for you, if you allow us to, and us doing it for you is the cosmos doing it for itself."

And I'd share those ideas with others and the words would flow through me, and it would feel so right and so true. But then when it came down to it in my life, I wasn't letting the dragons do that; I resisted them; I assumed I have to do everything by myself and that I couldn't call on them to support me. So even I didn't actually fully trust them and wasn't fully committed to our relationship.

So I got this tattoo as a symbol of my commitment. And now I can feel the connection growing stronger. I can kind of feel it on my skin, almost like the dragon energy is moving through me. And the dragons have told me how they are like arteries that flow the Kundalini, the lifeblood of the cosmos, through your body. And the dragon looks like he's made of ink that's flowing up my arm in that way. So, getting the tattoo made us come closer, and it was meaningful on many different levels.

Two-way communication

The Below is inviting you into a two-way relationship. Images, symbols, energies, and entities are communicating messages to you, but the Descent is not a passive process where you kick back and watch it unfold like a movie; it's an immersive world where you are invited (and, indeed, oftentimes forced) to fully participate.

There are a number of tips I can give you to help you to engage in two-way dialogue in order to enrich your immersion and deepen your communication. First and foremost, to echo Jeff's admonishment about solving a physics equation, I'll say that you should avoid interacting with the imaginal in ways that attempt to immediately interpret the mystery or collapse it into some kind of explanation. Let me paint two different scenarios:

First, an example of how to shut down or stifle the imaginal by leaping to conclusions. Imagine an angelic feminine form with hair made of radiant light emerges to you in a vision. She exudes joy, safety, and warmth, and you feel an intense attraction to her. When you emerge from your session, you jump online and do image searches for blonde goddesses. You discover a Norse goddess named Freyja who is said to be the goddess of love, and conclude that your vision must be a premonition of a new romantic adventure on the horizon.

Here's the second scenario, which is what actually happened when this feminine form appeared to me. The first time she visited, I spent a good amount of time just basking in her presence, feeling the emotions and body sensations she elicited in me. At the end of the session, I thanked her for coming to me and invited her to return if she wished to. And she did. At one point, after she had appeared to me a few times, I did some preliminary internet research, and I noted a number different goddesses with blonde hair. While I thought that she might be Freyja, because of the sensations of love and attraction, I didn't want to settle on that interpretation without more evidence.

Over time, this anonymous angelic figure appeared to me more often. I found her incredibly alluring, and wanted to engage with her more directly. So, in one drumming and spontaneous movement session, I opened up my visual and body-sensation channels and invited her into the space. I then stood silently, listening, watching, and feeling for a response. When I felt her presence emerge, I decided I would ask her for her name. I spoke out loud into the darkness of the practice area in my basement: "Freyja." I didn't feel anything change or shift. I repeated again, "Freyja." Still nothing.

I guessed that her name wasn't Freyja after all. Undaunted, I decided to go through the names of some of the other goddess names I had researched:

>"Frija" ... nothing.
>"Figg" ... nothing.
>"Ēostre" ... nothing.
>"Olwen" ... nothing.
>"Sunne" ... nothing.
>"Sol" ...

I kid you not, the instant I spoke that name (which means "sun" in Latin), a bright sun ray suddenly pierced through the single tiny window in my basement and streamed into the practice space. Whereas the whole place had been dark just a second ago, the rug I was standing on was now lit up with this sunbeam. I felt the goddess's presence fill my body more strongly than ever, an almost orgasmic sensation of bliss. Then, I heard her speak to me:

"Sol," she said ... "Sol. Sol. *Soul.*"

At that moment, the full meaning of her identity dawned on me (pun intended). She was a vision of the radiant light of my own soul, appearing to me in the shape of Sol, the Pagan goddess of the sun. My life was never the same after this revelation, and she has been a constant companion and reminder of my own divine essence.

I hope that these two scenarios clearly illustrate the difference between the kinds of actions that collapse the meaning of an imaginal event into a simplistic conclusion, versus those that invite more intimacy and relationality. I also hope to somehow convey the richness of the relationship you can have with the imaginal world if you focus on developing the two-way conversation instead of on "solving the mystery" or "figuring out what it all means" in a linear way. I never could have arrived at the complexity of this relationship with Sol by simply jumping to my own conclusions. I needed to let this imaginal being in, to get to know her by feel, to invite her into a conversation, and to allow a powerful synchronicity to take place in order for the full symbolic and emotional power of this imaginal vision to unfold. It required patience, time, curiosity, and presence to come to fruition.

Actually, though, the underlying principle is not all that complicated. Perhaps we could just say that the best advice is simply to treat imaginal beings as you would human people you encounter in ordinary life. If you met someone new that you were intrigued by, would you turn away from them in order to Google them on your phone and then make up your mind about who they are, or would you spend a little time chatting face to face in order to get to know them?

In the previous example, I had a two-way conversation with an imaginal being using words. But another really effective way of creating bidirectional communication with the imaginal world is to engage in physical acts of exchange. For me, the most effective way of doing that is to give offerings to specific entities, or groups of them, and to ask for blessings or other messages in return. But what do you offer to spirits?

When I first started out, I only gave two kinds of offerings: lighting candles and burning incense. This was because these two are extremely common offerings used in virtually all Asian religions (and quite a few non-Asian ones as well), and it seemed to me like the most logical place to start. However, once I began to get a bit more familiar with the Below, I began to branch out into more specific (and often, more spontaneous) gifts. I do sometimes look up traditional offerings to deities (e.g., marigolds for Virgin Mary), and do that if it feels right to me. However, for the most part, I just ask them what kinds of offerings they prefer.

This was yet another arena in which I had to learn to listen with an open mind to what was being said, instead of imposing my own thoughts and opinions onto the Below. One time, for example, I had a particularly vivid vision of the spirit I call "La Vieja," an elderly Indigenous South American woman who advises me on how to make connections with my Indigenous ancestors. In this vision, I visited her in her home in the underworld. Sitting in a rocking chair, she puffed on a huge cigar, the smoke encircling her head and filling the room. She tapped the ashes out into the smiling mouth of a skull, which clacked its teeth like it was enjoying eating the spent tobacco. The scene then changed to an image of me, carrying a tobacco pouch at my waist. It was clear to me that the message La Vieja was imparting was that I should use tobacco offerings for my ancestors.

To be honest, my first reaction to this idea was that I must be making things up! It felt like I must be mixing my own stereotyped ideas about Indigenous people using ceremonial tobacco into my visions. Plus, I had no interest in smoking or even having tobacco in my home. But, as I had done in the past, I decided to not reject the message outright before sitting with the idea for a bit. So I sat with it. I also started doing some research, and I soon realized that, while I had always associated tobacco offerings with Indigenous North Americans, the tobacco plant is actually native to Mesoamerica, and is/was used widely by all kinds of Indigenous healers and ritualists in most parts of South America, including in the areas where my ancestors are from. Upon further reflection, I also remembered three facts that tied tobacco to my own ancestral bloodlines: (1) there was an ancestor on my maternal grandmother's side who worked as a cigar roller, (2) my maternal grandfather worked for a cigarette company for almost his whole life, and (3) my father was a nicotine addict and died of emphysema.

Adding all of this together, in the end, I concluded that La Vieja was right: tobacco was actually the perfect offering for my ancestors. Once I had this realization, I purchased pure, natural tobacco leaves and began burning a small amount in a bowl on my home altar as part of the closing of my daily ritual. I immediately felt that my ancestors were quite happy with this, and it made me feel more connected to them. The point of my story is that I never would have thought of tobacco offerings myself; this insight could only have come from a two-way dialogue with the Below.

Aside from directly addressing them by making offerings, another way of enhancing two-way communication that I have found works well for me is to use oracle decks. I've never been into Tarot or other commercially available cards because their symbolism doesn't have any deep meaning for me. However, as I continued to have highly meaningful encounters with different entities and energies during my Descent, I began to create 3×3 printed cards with names and images I felt were evocative of my own personal imaginal lexicon. I made a card each for Bachué, María, Kuan Yin, Sol, La Vieja, the jaguar, other animal and angelic spirits, ancestral guides, the four elements, and others—about sixty in total.

While I continued to engage with this whole range of entities through my visions, journeys, offerings, and other ritual practices, I now had an additional method of receiving messages—another channel aside from the sensory ones I had been working with—that could also enrich my communication. I incorporated using the deck into my morning practice. After burning the tobacco, I would shuffle the deck and draw a card. Sometimes I would ask a specific question first. Usually I considered the card I drew to be a message about something I needed to focus on or attend to that day. Each of the cards had a wide range of symbolic meanings, emotional connotations, and other associations built up from my experiences in visions and rituals in addition to the specific visual details in the images. This meant that the messages received from the cards could come through in a wide variety of ways.

My point, again, is to use tools that open up the possibilities for conversation, connection, and relationship instead of shutting down or collapsing the conversation. I'm not saying that you have to use oracle cards specifically. Friends of mine use mandalas, paintings, natural objects, homemade ritual implements, or all kinds of other things. Think about what kinds of tools *you* can employ to bring in additional sensory domains and material objects in order to enrich your communications with the Below.

In the long run, the goal is to establish meaningful reciprocal relationships with our imaginal interlocutors. In time, these relationships can be every bit as rich and as real as those between humans. Listen to how Misha made one of the most important connections in her life with the spirit tree outside her home:

> In the middle of the night, there was some kind of real emotional need happening for me, and I just felt called to go out to be with this Arizona ash tree outside my house. This one is the first tree I planted on this land. And, I had put in a lot of effort to make a really good home for this tree to root into. At some point, I figured out that even though it has flowers, it's male. I didn't know its sex before that.
>
> Anyway, on that moonlit night I go out to the tree. And you know, I'm just following my sense of whatever needs to happen. So, I'm hugging him and I've got some low branches that are trimmed in ways so birds can sit without having foliage in their way. And I put my hands on some of these low branches and it feels very supportive. I don't remember exactly the specifics, but I was asking him for help in a very heartfelt, vulnerable way. And I felt like he volunteered—or I don't know the right languaging for it—but, somehow we got married that night. He became my spirit husband.
>
> And, a name came to me through some kind of audible inner hearing—as if it were sound but I just knew the name. It said "Ashleigh." And I was like, "Oh, of course. Right."
>
> And, when I go out and hug him sometimes now, I have the front of my body toward his trunk, and then his energy comes around behind and then into my heart center, and it's like, he's hugging me through me. Anyway, it feels really strange to talk about my husband the ash tree. It feels that there's something non-ordinary and very sacred about that. And the whole connecting process was spontaneous; I was just following what was needed and where I intuited to position my body.
>
> One part of it that is really touching for me is that it was almost like a form of reciprocity, but not as in a transactional way. He was like, "You put in all this energy, you gave me a home, a place to be. You've cared for me all these decades. Now, I can care for you."

I guess I feel like he sensed what kind of need I was expressing when I was asking for help. That was kind of like a call into the void. It was an undifferentiated kind of a call. So it's as if he stepped forward, you know, and just knew deeply what was needed.

And, another piece of it was that I felt called to cut off a couple of smaller branches. The sense was that I could carve wooden beads from one of them, so that I would have a rosary or a mala that's beads from his wood that he gave to me. Then that would become a new ritual object that's infused with all this meaning and context and relationality. With the other branch, I could carve pieces to give out to individuals who I do healing work for. In this way, his healing presence could move out more broadly into the world and extend the web of relationship.

Meaningfulness

In some forms of spirituality, the mind is demonized and blamed for all of our suffering. But, as I've stated throughout this book, the process of Descent into the Below is the process of liberating every part of you to fully be itself. The mind is no different than any other autonomous component of your sacred wholeness. Thinking is a natural capacity of the brain, and its activities are pretty much beyond our control. As such, there is no need to silence thoughts, any more than there is a need to silence sounds or visions or other sensory phenomena.

It might be useful to tamp down the mind and the senses for a time, while on a meditation retreat for example, in order to achieve certain psychedelic effects or rarified states of consciousness. But, sooner or later, thinking returns, and there's nothing wrong with that. Where there is a problem, however, is in believing that thinking is the whole picture. Rational thinking offers one perspective on things, but we should never imagine that is the final word. This is particularly important when engaging with the Below.

The mind is constantly taking in the raw data of our experience, and weaving it together into webs of connotations, implications, memories, and plans for the future. Because it is constantly doing this, it is unavoidable that your mind will have a lot to say about the entities, energies, and events you encounter in the Below. The mind will want to know what's going on and why, how to categorize and label it, how what's happening now connects with the past and what it means for the future, and so on and so forth. The mind might try to explain away imaginal phenomena, try to attenuate your Descent, or even shut down the process entirely. Or, if it is really taken aback by an experience it can't figure out, the mind can kick up a lot of fear, rumination, doubt, and other thought-loops that can be experienced as negative or troubling. At the far end of this spectrum, panic, paranoia, and existential terror are all products of a mind that can't find its familiar footing.

In order to survive the Descent, part of what we need to learn to do is to live in the ambiguous liminal space of not knowing. That is not to say, however, that the mind has no role to play in engaging with the Below. The mind is actually a very important tool when used properly: not to explain, but to create meaningfulness.

What's the difference? Explanation is reductive and linear while meaning-making is associative and opens up possibilities. As an example of how each kind of thinking changes your experience, consider the following imaginal event.

For several weeks I had been seeing in visions an image of myself, riding on the back of my jaguar guide, carrying a little red bag. In each hand I wielded a sword made of quartz crystals. The two glowed brightly and lit my way through the darkness of the underworld.

One day, I was looking through some old possessions of mine, and I came across a little red "mojo bag" full of magical implements that my late grandmother had given me decades ago when I was a teenager. Inside, there was a small sword-shaped quartz crystal. A few weeks later, I was cleaning out the incense pot I was using for altar offerings, taking out the rocks and rinsing them with water. There, among the rocks, I found a second, identical quartz sword. I have no idea where it came from or how it got there.

Those are the facts. Now, let's see how two different kinds of thinking can weave radically different interpretations out of them. First, let's use linear thinking to *explain* these events. One line of linear reasoning is that I must have subconsciously remembered the quartz crystals being in those locations, and then those memories must have influenced my vision. Another linear explanation might be that my grandmother must have sent me the crystals to use in my practice. This kind of thinking is reductionistic: its purpose is to decide on an answer to the question of why something happened. It wants to choose which explanation is the right one. That is to say, its purpose is to limit the possibilities of the thing being explained, to eliminate the mystery and to come to a firm conclusion about "what's really going on."

In contrast, let's see how associative thinking would unpack the same events. Here, for example, I might reflect upon the connection between my vision and the crystals I found and allow my thoughts to wander a bit. There might be a lot of thoughts running through my mind about this, but I don't have to give too much credence to any one of them. Amid that mental noise, there may be some gems that I feel like cogitating on for a bit. For example, I may realize that the red bag my grandmother gave me decades ago, in addition to the crystal, also contained a number of other magical implements related to guidance and protection. It included, for example, a miniature compass and pocket knife, as well as a tiny Buddha image. Perhaps, I think, the quartz crystal in my vision could be associated with these other objects and their meanings, thus not only with lighting my way, but also giving me guidance, strength, and protection?

Another thought perhaps arises that the grandmother who gave me this crystal "sword" was herself a practitioner of Chinese martial arts—and sometimes used a sword in her own daily practice. Maybe there's something important here about continuity between the generations in our practice of Asian spiritual traditions. Come to think of it, she died within a few months of me rediscovering the mojo bag. Could the quartz have represented a "passing of the baton" from her to me? An invitation for her to guide and mentor me in my spiritual questing from the afterlife? Speaking of that, I've never used a sword, staff, or similar tool in my own movement practice. What would that be like?

Now, what about the other crystal, the one from the incense pot? I've burned incense in offerings for ancestral spirits many times, so that's reinforcing the ancestral connection. But, I've also used it for other purposes, such as honoring the other goddesses I pray to. Speaking of goddesses, I remember that my wife has a protective quartz amulet of Kuan Yin that was given to her while we were traveling in Asia. Is there a special connection between Kuan Yin and quartz crystals?

I hop online to research this question, and start delving deeper into the associations of quartz crystals in other traditions around the world. Again, I'm not clinging to any particular piece of information, but just gathering more associations. I read that quartzes are widely used by spiritual practitioners for their empowering and cleansing properties. I discover that they are said to be the strongest crystals in certain shamanic traditions. I read more about their traditional and modern uses in order to further inform myself about the powers my imaginal sword might possess.

Notice that the point here isn't to figure out "what's really going on" or even to dwell on whether or not these associated ideas I am collecting are true. The goal is to generate more and more potentials, more and more layers of connotations, which in turn can pack the event with richer and richer meaningfulness. Far from landing on a single explanation, as my linear mind wanted to me to, through this process of association, the event now comes to be entangled in a web of connotations having to do with my childhood, ancestors, goddesses, spiritual practices, and a global web of symbols of protection, illumination, enlightenment, and connection.

Best of all, because the mind is a meaning-making machine running essentially automatically, all this associative thinking happened with minimal effort. All I had to do was steer my mind away from jumping to linear explanatory conclusions, and keep it on the associative track. (For some people, journaling might help with maintaining this mindset.)

One kind of conclusion that the linear mind seems to especially like to jump to is to answer definitively the question of whether or not these mysterious imaginal phenomena are real. But, answering these questions in any definitive way is a linear explanation that shuts down the possibilities inherent in the experience. If you decide that the Below is actually a product of your own psychology, then that will limit your experience in certain ways; if you decide it's actually coming from some external source (particular deities, astral realms, aliens, or what have you), then that will limit your experience in other ways. Instead of letting your mind jump to explanatory conclusions, can you just sit in the unknown, and let the fullness of the mystery unfold? Set your mind to deepening the mystery by unpacking it in more and more meaningfulness, but don't let it settle on any one detail as the ultimate answer. You'll find that the meaningfulness of the Below evolves and deepens through a process of ongoing unfolding, exploration, and discovery.

Experimentation and innovation

In general, the approach to the Below I am advocating is experimental and innovative. You pay attention to opening your sensory channels. You follow your guides and trust where they lead you. You get sponteneously inspired or search through books and existing spiritual teachings for ideas about specific techniques to try. When you find something that interests you, you take it up, implementing some version of the practice for a few weeks or months, in order to see what effect it has on the quality, intensity, and impact of your experience of the Below. If you notice something working, you tweak it further to enhance the effects. You discard whatever doesn't work, and you keep experimenting with adding new practices you think might be promising. You might start clustering certain practices that work well together into "modules" that can be done in a particular sequence at a particular time of day. You maintain a regular, rhythmic structure to your practice while also allowing for plenty of flexibility and innovation. All along, you pay attention to grounding and integration with daily life.

In my case, when I began my Descent, I already had a morning routine in place where I sat in meditation out on my back deck for about an hour and then practiced qigong for half an hour. Additionally, I did an hour of walking meditation at the end of my work day and did yoga in the evening before bed. Once I started the Descent in earnest, I realized that it was during my qigong practice that I experienced an enhanced receptivity to visions. So, I started to experiment with that portion of my routine to see how I could maximize those effects. Little by little, as a result of these experiments, my qigong session started to transform.

By the time my Descent finished three years later, that half hour of qigong had become a completely different module. It had moved to my basement and had gradually morphed into a forty or forty-five minute session, the first half involving shamanic drumming and vigorous spontaneous movements where I allowed spirits and energies to arise and move through my body, and the second half involving sitting in the center of a visualized mandala surrounded by ancestors and protective goddesses on all sides. Often, those spirits took me on a journey to faraway imaginal worlds where I met teachers and other beneficial beings.

Over time, I also developed a small altar that I used for fifteen or twenty minutes or so to initiate and complete the morning module. Some of the things I incorporated into these rituals that opened and closed my morning module included ringing a bell to invoke beneficial deities; my surrender prayer; offerings of food, drink, and tobacco for my ancestors; offering of fire, light, and perfume to my spirit guides; consulting an oracle card for divination.

For me, it happened to be the morning module where I incorporated most of my Below-centered practices, and I fit a whole range of different practices into that time. I kept the things that worked for me, but I let go of many of the ones I tried—such as dream journaling, chanting mantras, a martial-arts type exercise routine, high-heat sauna, and making art, among others—when I saw that they didn't enhance my experience of the Below in any kind of notable way.

As I keep saying, I am not giving you these details to suggest that my style of practice is the right way for you to do things. Experiment and do what works for you. I just want to give an example of how rituals might be incorporated, adapted, and stitched together as a part of a process of creative innovation. The main idea here is that nothing should be fixed in stone. Spiritual teachings—no matter how authoritative they may be—are merely suggestions, rough guidelines that you can feel free to tweak or ignore as you see fit. All of your practices should be flexible, adjustable, modifiable, and you are the one who is in the drivers' seat.

Your best source for the design of your own personalized suite of ritual practices is always going to be your own inner guidance. That may come as a gut feeling, or a felt sense of alignment and purpose, or an energetic pull toward something, or even in the form of a seemingly external spirit protector, guide, or higher power. (Note that inner guidance doesn't come from thinking, emotions, or other egoic activity.) Whatever form your guidance comes in, if it's authentic, it will always lead you to make innovations in your practice that are beneficial.

When you are familiar with what practices work for you and help you to connect with the Below, and you are communicating well with your inner guidance, you will feel confident to spontaneously modify or invent rituals on the fly, knowing that they will be effective and meaningful. I have been called upon to do this many times in a variety of circumstances over the years, but I still remember one of the first times as particularly meaningful.

I was staying in a cottage beside a small private lake, and one day found myself alone for several hours around sunset. I had been feeling a certain draw toward the lake, and took the opportunity to try to connect with its elemental spirits in a more intentional way than I had done up to that point. I didn't know what I was going to do to connect, but I knew I wanted to go into the water to do so.

Stripping down to bare skin, I entered the lake up to my waist and looked out over the water, watching the ripples of orange and pink light rays dancing across its surface. I noticed that, because I was moving, these ripples were traveling from me outward, emanating out toward the center of the lake. So, I imagined that these ripples were carrying my good intentions and energies out to the water spirits, bringing them messages of joy and well-being. As I stilled my body and relaxed my breathing, I watched as the ripple patterns slowly changed across the quiet surface of the lake. After a while, they were no longer emanating outwards, but were instead coming from the center of the lake towards me. I thanked the spirits for returning my message, and I felt a subtle sense of pleasure on my skin as the ripples lapped gently at my torso.

I was moved to make an offering to the lake spirits to embody my gratitude and respect for them, but here I was, naked, waist-deep in water, with nothing to give them. Just then, I remembered that my body is itself about 70 percent water. In other words, the water spirits that I was communicating with out there in the lake were also here within my own body! Having had this realization, the offering I should make suddenly became clear. I urinated, visualizing the waters of my body intermingling with the waters of the lake. Then, I dunked my head under the surface so that the waters of the lake washed over the waters of my body. The intention was a commingling, or unification, of the water spirits of my body with those of the lake.

As I stood back up after this exchange of elements, I noticed that I was now surrounded by dozens of flower-like plants. My movements as I dunked myself must have disturbed the underwater foliage of the lake, causing these to float up to the surface. Given the context, it was clear to me that this was a positive response from the water spirits, a confirmation that my invented ritual and offering was well received and a celebration of our unity.

Now, if I just had told you, without further context, that I urinated in a lake to honor the water spirits that inhabited it, you might think I was disrespectful, or crazy, or both. But, in the moment, I hope you see how this made total sense. Anyway, the point of my story is not to prescribe the best way for you to communicate with water spirits. It's to give you an example of how ritual innovation can take shape spontaneously. In that moment, standing in the lake, I was deeply immersed in the imaginal world and had a sincere intention to connect. I had given offerings and exchanged energies with many types of spirits in the past, and was confident about my ability to feel into the situation at hand and to respond appropriately. With those things in place, the connection could unfold naturally and I could respond spontaneously in an authentic way with actions that felt right and were meaningful in the moment.

Notice that I didn't consult a guidebook on how to construct a ritual for the water element. I didn't need to pull out my phone and Google what kind of gift to offer to a lake spirit. I didn't even reach into my own repertoire of rituals I had cultivated and perfected over the years. The key is not figuring out "the right thing to do." It's about creating your own authentic relationship with the Below, and then taking guidance from the energies that emerge through that connection.

Here's another story with a similar point, this time about how Jack sought and followed the advice of his dragon guides when he was in need of financial assistance:

> When I first was starting my business, and was having financial problems, I reached out to the golden dragon, and I was like, "Please help me. I really, really need your help." And she was like, "Of course." So I said, "Okay, what do we need to do? Do we need to do a ritual or something?" And she's like, "Yeah, we can do a ritual." And I'm like, "Okay, so do I need to offer you money? Like, do you want all the rest of my money?" And she's like, "No, you don't need to think like that. I just love really shiny coins. I don't care about the value, I just like that it's shiny. So, take a few pennies that are super shiny, take them down to the water by the sea. Place them on a stone that feels right for you. Ask me to provide you wealth. And it's done."
>
> And so I go down to the sea. And there's a huge storm, and the waves are enormous. I go down to the water and there were a couple of stones that were already on top of each other. It looked like a little altar. So I walk over to that, and I place my coins on it. I state my wish. And then I look up and there's this huge wave coming towards me. So I run out of the way so that I don't get wet.
>
> And as I turn around, I see the wave coming in and it goes over my offering and then pulls it back into the sea. This was pretty mind-blowing to see. And then I look out over the ocean and I could just feel the dragon's spirit all throughout the ocean. Like she's just this huge, vast being. It felt amazing. I felt really uplifted by it.
>
> And, within about two days, I had a sale for my most expensive long-term program that brought in more money than I had ever brought in a single sale. And it completely wrote off my debts and provided for me for the next three months.

Microcosms

One effective way of enhancing connection and communication with the Below is to symbolize or embody it in physical form. For many people, the most natural way of doing this is to create an altar. By "altar" I don't mean any particular traditional configuration. I really just mean a dedicated place where you keep a collection of imaginal objects, images, implements, and other material symbols or representations of the Below.

My own altar (Figure 5) is actually on a small chest of drawers. In them I have collected feathers gifted to me by vulture spirits, various charms and amulets, sets of mala beads, and various other meaningful objects and implements from throughout my Descent. In other drawers I have tea-light candles, sage and palo santo incense, tobacco and whiskey for the ancestors, and various small cups and vessels for making other offerings. On top of the chest, there is a circle of small statues representing my animal guides, some ashes from my grandparents' cremation, and other objects representing other ancestors. Standing above them, statues and framed images of María and Kuan Yin, and a photo

Figure 5. My microcosm.

of Rómulo Rozo's Bachué, and a vase with a white flower symbolizing Sol. In between and among these figures, there's a candle, a bell, a small bowl of tobacco, a bowl of stones for incense, and a lighter.

You know from reading this book that these objects capture many of the major themes of my imaginal world. However, it's more than just a haphazard collection of objects: my altar is also a microcosm. Etymologically, the word microcosm means "miniature cosmos," and the objects on my altar are indeed laid out in such a way that they represent the structure of my imaginal universe. Having these objects laid out in this configuration allows me to engage with them in highly meaningful ways, and doing so routinely triggers the emergence of certain experiences and realizations. Of course, I can have imaginal experiences anywhere. But, I find that I am often transported into a more open state of mind just by standing in front of the altar. As I light candles and make offerings to each of the entities represented there, I feel my channels opening up further and further.

While to me it is a mandala that captures complex relationships between the elements of my imaginal world, the layout of my altar is more complex and therefore the logic behind its structure is a bit hard to explain. My friend Jeff has a much simpler example of a microcosmic altar that you can quickly grasp. This comes from his blog on August 7, 2020 (condensed and lightly edited by me), in which he describes how he created an altar in his art studio to visually encapsulate the three parts of what he calls his "self-sense." These three elements are "little jeffy," which is his mundane everyday ego-self; "Big Jeff," his creative self that is plugged into the imaginal realm; and "The Unborn," which he also calls "the world of Mysterious Rapture." In the language of this book, I believe that these three terms are referring to the Middle, Below, and the Above respectively.

> To put it simply, ritual has come to increasingly define how I approach even the simplest of activities. This hasn't come about by conscious intention; rather, it seems to have gradually grown into the fabric of my activities without my noticing, until one day it dawned on me what had happened.
>
> One of the rituals I've developed consists of a small altar just inside the door of my working studio. Central to the altar is a Tibetan singing bowl, one with a rich sound and long period of resonance. Next to it is a hand-wrought wooden handle wrapped at the end with fabric, for the purpose of striking the bowl. Arranged in front

of the bowl are three images on postcards of artworks of mine, each image representing for me one of the three holons that make up the holarchy of my self-sense—little jeffy; Big Jeff; The Unborn.

When I've settled into my studio for a day of work, before any creative activity begins, I perform a benediction of sorts—I first place a hand on the image representing little jeffy, acknowledge his place in the holarchy and the value he brings, then I strike the bowl, focusing intently on the reverberating sound as it slowly fades. Then I follow suit with Big Jeff, and follow that with The Unborn. Finally I strike the bowl and stretch both hands over all of the images, acknowledging the holarchy of my self-sense and its structure that holds it all together. All of this is a very centering, very calming ritualistic start to my creative day.

Jeff's altar is a microcosm that symbolizes the Above, Middle, and Below, and allows for a ritual that unifies this "holarchy" (i.e., wholes that are also parts of something larger) through the medium of sound. For Jeff, striking the singing bowl serves as a daily reminder that he is more than just a one-dimensional being, and helps him drop in and open up to his full self as he begins to work on his art each day.

While altars are microcosms that are intentionally designed as a dedicated space for ritual practice, other kinds of spaces or objects can also be microcosms. For example, I have a tattoo on my right arm that is a microcosm, combining potent imaginal symbols of the Above, Middle, and Below into a coherent diagram or representation of the unity of the three.

For me, however, the most powerfully evocative microcosm of all is that statue of Bachué by Rozo. She is my "axis mundi," the imaginal center of the universe around which the Earth and the Heavens spin. I don't expect the image in Figure 3 to affect you as it does me—or even to have any impact at all. However, I would invite you to take a look back at it and to notice how, at the top of the statue, Bachué is a sun goddess. Her perfectly equanimous face emits rays of light, while her arms extend upwards in a cone of heavenly light that streams down from Above. As our eye moves downward, she transforms into a human figure. Here, she is a sensual embodied being with heaving breasts and undulating hips. She is a lover and a mother, an incarnate being of flesh and blood. Moving further down, she transforms yet again as her serpentine coils lead us into the dark waters of the underworld, churning and frothing with snakes. To me, she is the full package, from the Void to the Abyss, and everything in between.

Paranormal abilities

People talk a lot about paranormal abilities emerging spontaneously during an awakening process. Some people consciously try to acquire or develop such abilities. Some traditions hold that the emergence of these powers is an important marker of spiritual attainment, and some even say that not having them means you are not awakened. Conversely, the Buddha is famous for saying that all such powers are a distraction, or even a perversion of spirituality. Here, I'll offer you my thoughts, which is a different take than any of those positions.

I agree that it seems to be the case that all sorts of paranormal effects can occur when you are navigating the Below. I think of these effects as falling onto a spectrum. On one end of the spectrum, uncanny or weird events can be associated with certain states of consciousness. These may be paranormal, but they don't have profound spiritual meanings. For example, in my own experience, I developed for a period of a few months extraordinarily strong powers of smell. In Misha's case, she sometimes experiences weirdness with electrical appliances:

> If my energy gets too intense, into a "screechy" kind of frequency, it interferes with electronics. I have this one particular CD player that, if the energy gets too screechy, will pause the CD until I calm the energy down enough, and then it starts playing again from exactly where it was paused. And it can happen with Zoom as well.
>
> It also happens with this one friend. I don't know why, but it's something about her technology. So that when my energy starts getting screechy, then she starts having problems with hearing me through her device. This doesn't happen with other people's phones, but just with that one particular person's phone.
>
> So, yeah, I can interfere with electronic devices, although I don't do it on purpose. That would be kind of a nice party trick if I could do it on purpose, right?

Beyond these meaningless kinds of effects, there are also those paranormal abilities that can be considered gifts or blessings. These are often called *siddhis*, using a Sanskrit word meaning "accomplishment."

Jack talked with me about some of the kinds of powers or abilities that he has discovered and developed through his process of awakening the Below:

> I guess one of the funny things with the whole awakening experience is that when things start to open up, they become very ordinary very quickly. So, something that someone else might think is a siddhi, I might not even have realized or conceptualized in that way.
>
> Like, I can see divine light, this golden white light, shining out of every object, every human being, everything. And, what I learned after a few years of seeing that was that when human beings are baring their soul, this light shines more brightly. And if I focus on it with an open heart and a lot of presence, it will shine more brightly. It's like I help people to heal by holding their spirit with my spirit, but through my eyes. Just by seeing them, they become unburdened and their soul shines more brightly. So you could call that a siddhi. I use it for the healing of others, and I benefit by being healed and opened at the same time.
>
> There's also the beings that I channel: some people might say that's a siddhi to be able to communicate with deities and dragons. And to allow them to occupy my body and flow through my body, and to speak to people through me. To be a link between their world and the human world. And I deliver messages from them to support people who are listening to me, and to do healing work with other people. And I can feel them expanding my consciousness too. They'll focus in on a trauma held inside of the body of the person I'm working with, and then expand the field of consciousness so that I can sense where that trauma links to past lifetimes or other points in time and space. So that the trauma isn't just held in this body in this moment in time, it now links to all moments in time and space. That, you could say, is a siddhi that I'm using to help people heal.
>
> And then, there's manifesting prosperity, which some people also would call a siddhi. The dragons I channel also are deities of wealth. They would be like, "Jack, you do realize that in all of the stories, we sleep on piles of gold, right? There's a reason for that!" It's all about flows of energy. You are this whole cosmos and this whole earth, and that's where all abundance flows from. All abundance that anyone can ever have, it always flows from the

cosmos and from the earth, and it flows through energy channels. So, if you are blocking the channels of abundance that exist inside your body with shame or trauma, you are blocking the flow of the earth and you are blocking the flow of the cosmos. So by unblocking it, by allowing the cosmos and the earth to provide for you, you are allowing the cosmos and the earth to flow, you are undamming a river. That siddhi is a gift for the cosmos, for the earth, and for yourself.

In my opinion, there's nothing wrong with courting synchronicity, premonition, or blessings in your life like the ones Jack is describing. There's also nothing wrong with asking higher powers, ancestors, and other spirit guardians for guidance, help, or support—whether with spiritual matters or with mundane things like money or a job. But, I do believe it is a perversion of spirituality and an enormous karmic fault if you ever use siddhis you gained from your spiritual practice for greedy ends or to harm others.

That is why, in my opinion, if you start moving in the direction of cultivating paranormal powers—either intentionally or spontaneously—it is imperative to take responsibility to ensure that any powers you develop are used to benefit and never to harm others. Therefore, I think your first act of magic should be to place a permanently limiting spell on yourself that will prevent any siddhi you ever gain in the future from possibly ever bringing suffering to another being. At the same time, you should vow that any power you do gain, if you ever tried to use it for unenlightened purposes, would be immediately rendered ineffectual. With that limiting spell in place, then I think you can invite siddhis that will benefit all beings to emerge and to flow through you, as necessary, in order to help where needed. Set the intention and forget it. You need not cultivate any specific powers, but just see what arises naturally to meet the needs of the moment. And, whatever does arise, don't ever cling to it as it moves through you. Remember that it's never about you; it's only ever about spreading love and alleviating suffering.

Another thing you don't want to get hung up on is figuring out whether paranormal powers are real. As I've said now many times, you'll do best to abandon that whole line of thinking, since any specific answer to the question will only serve to limit the possibilities of the mystery.

Emptying your vessel

While we are not demonizing the mind in this book, sometimes it's important to be able to set aside thinking in order to allow something else to flow through us. In this section, I am going to talk about a whole spectrum of experiences that includes artistic creativity, channeling, mediumship, trance, and possession. I think of all of these phenomena as variations on the common theme of "emptying the vessel." That is to say, they are all examples of what happens when you are able to set aside your thinking mind and allow the unimpeded flow of imaginal energies to emerge, flow through your being, and emanate out into the world.

Here's Jeff again, talking about how tapping into these energies has become a central part of his creative process as an artist. This is from his blog on February 27, 2012 (as always, extracted and slightly edited by me):

> For some artists, engaging in the practice of art-making leads them to an exploration of subconscious and unconscious territories of the psyche. When this happens one finds that the unconscious—that which, by definition, was unavailable to conscious attention—is far richer and deeper and wider than was anticipated. This is certainly true of the personal unconscious ... but there is another realm of the psyche that can become available to creative exploration—the elusive, sometimes mysterious, sometimes scary, always surprising transpersonal unconscious.
>
> It's here that creativity starts tapping into energies never imagined and rarely understood. From far below the region of the personal unconscious, the deep unconscious reveals species instincts and urges that are so raw and formless they can barely be contained in cultural symbols, yet manage to find creative form in myth and ritual that is often shimmering in numinosity ...
>
> It's infinite, unlimited, endless, awe inspiring. This is where the artist in his/her creative practice finally stops seeking and begins to be guided. This is where the artist steps through doors never before recognized into territories never before intuited. This is where the artist steps back from the work, looks at it and wonders, "Who the hell did that?"
>
> This is where I am. And how I got here is mostly a mystery to me, though in looking back I see a long and battered journey that

was somehow fueled and inspired by a crazy intuition, a pull from far off, dimly perceived but undeniable.

An artist engaging with "the transpersonal unconscious"—by which I think Jeff means the Below—must find a way to take their everyday Middle-world ego-selves (their "little jeffies") out of the driver's seat. They must instead embrace not knowing, trust in the process that is spontaneously unfolding, and allow surprising new things to emerge out of the mystery. That is precisely the same thing that the medium does when channeling. Whereas the artist allows the mystery to manifest through the pencil, paint, or clay—or in Jeff's case, string—the channeler's raw materials are words. The medium empties themselves out and allows words to autonomously come to life and to flow through them.

Again, where you think those words are coming from doesn't matter. Whatever you think the source is—the "transpersonal unconscious," spirits, deities, the Akashic Record, etc.—the thing you must do is the same: you must find a way to empty yourself out and allow the information that is emerging to move through unimpeded.

Here's Jack talking about his experience with emptying out his vessel:

> I was preparing to come to England to give these talks and lead my first day-long retreat. And in my mind, I was thinking, "I need to prepare for this. I need to have things written down. I need to know what I'm doing." And the dragons came in and they were like, "No, no, do not do that. You need to do this spontaneously. It needs to come straight from your heart. And you need to learn that you can trust yourself and trust life enough to step into this."
>
> And then what happened was my flights got canceled at the last minute, and it created a lot of stress. I was totally busy with all of that, and I didn't have time to even think about what I was going to do. And then I arrived at the venue right before I was supposed to go on. I arrived, got introduced, and then it was like, "Okay, Jack, the next hour and forty-five minutes are yours. Off you go!"
>
> And, I did it. You know, I trusted it. I just said what was coming through my heart at the moment. I channeled the beings when they came through. And everything came through spontaneously.
>
> What's necessary is stepping away from the mind and trusting. I go into a trance state, and I trust in the beings that I'm connected to,

> because I've built a relationship with them over time, and they've proven themselves trustworthy. And then my consciousness is in the background. My humanity is in the background, and I let them be in the foreground.

Are there specific instructions on how to empty your vessel and let the energies flow? In Jeff's case, we already know that he has a microcosmic altar in his studio and a daily ritual that helps him to plug into his full self before he begins work. In my case, I often do not need to do anything other than step into the right context and the flow starts happening spontaneously. But, often, it helps to give a little nudge in the desired direction. For example, if you want to channel words, just start writing or speaking a bit in a spontaneous way; if you want to bring in creative inspiration, just start putting the pencil to the page or the paint onto the canvas.

In writing this book, for example, I have felt that every word has been channeled. All I have needed to do is to open up the laptop, start typing a sentence, and then something takes over. My fingers start flying over the keyboard and the words just come to life of their own accord. While the channeled information is pouring out of me, I am totally plugged in and almost oblivious to my surroundings. And, yet, it is totally effortless: I'm looking at the display on my screen right now telling me I have written nearly 10,000 words in the last two days. Tomorrow, I'll spend some time going back and reading what I've written here, and it will seem to me like I had little if anything to do with this creation. (As Jeff said, "Who the hell did that?")

Misha has a more concrete and intentional technique she uses to empty her vessel:

> The first thing that comes to mind for me is putting the body in an open receptive posture. Lying on my back, neutral posture, symmetrical position, palms up, open and allowing. And then internally, do the same thing with the mind and the attitude, so that's also open and receptive. And then, allowing—and maybe even sometimes inviting—whatever wants to come forward in experience. I'm intuitively sensing into that which wants to come forward, but not in a directive way where I'm trying to find something specific. And then, paying attention. When something starts showing up, allowing it to continue, mainly by just resting the attention

on what's happening in the physical sensations and energy fields. Occasionally there's an inner prompting to more actively encourage a process to emerge. So, very highly attentive and attuned to what's showing up in this moment as it's emerging.

Don't try to compare it against anything. Don't try to make meaning out of it. Don't try to analyze it. Notice in a very fluid in-the-moment way, like a seismographic sensor as the page of experience is going underneath it, noticing experiences flowing by.

And once there's an energy moving, if it's sufficiently present, if it's becoming more stable in its expression, then sometimes, there's an intuitive sense to accentuate something. Like, maybe there's an arching of the neck and maybe letting a deep growl out to accentuate it. And that can really help it to come forward and more fully express. There could be more body movements and vocalizations. Even, you know, gnashing of teeth and stuff like that. There can also be some vocalizations that express feelings, like, "Oh, this is yummy," or, "Yay, relaxation!" And there are other energies that also are more vulnerable with vocalizations more like whimpering. When that's going on, it can be the full body that's being moved. And I'm not deciding anything. The energy is moving the body and causing the vocalizations.

While Misha's tools are entirely internal, in my experience, there are also external aids that can significantly enhance the emptying of the vessel. For me, I discovered that putting on a shamanic drum track and allowing my body to move spontaneously in my darkened practice space can sometimes nudge me into a full trance state where my body deva or some other protector or guide will take control of my body.

In these kinds of situations, do we want to give over complete control or remain partially present? I think the answer to this question is individual. If you don't feel that you are drawn to full possession naturally, then there's no reason to think that kind of experience is a required feature of awakening the Below. However, if you do find yourself wanting to vacate your vessel spontaneously, you can welcome that as part of your process. With your eyes wide open about the potential risks and rewards, and making sure you're not opening yourself up to random influences, go ahead and open your sensory channels even wider than you did previously and invite your guides and protectors to "take the steering wheel."

In all cases, in order to empty your vessel, you need to suspend your judgment, interpretation, and other critical faculties, and just let things flow. If nothing happens, or it's not a very deep trance, keep at it and experiment with different aspects of the set and setting. I think you'll find that this is a skill that anyone can cultivate. What happens when you do—creativity, channeling, mediumship, trance, possession, or something else altogether—you won't necessarily be able to predict or control. As with everything else in the Below, if your guides and protectors are leading the way, then you can trust that you can just surrender to what is happening and allow it to unfold naturally.

Establishing and maintaining boundaries

Navigating the Below in a way that is both safe and responsible requires a strong commitment to ethics. As we have been discussing throughout this book, surrendering yourself to the Below involves the ego totally giving over control to the autonomy of your body, spirits, energies, the natural world, and a host of other agents. What these facets of your being present to you can be quite surprising—shocking, even. It is therefore advisable to have strong ethical commitments in place in advance, which can act like guardrails on the Descent.

In my view, a firm line should always be drawn at the point where your newfound freedom may possibly bring harm to another being. Awakening the Below leads to the liberation of every facet of the cosmos, and there is no way that is compatible with you harming another being. If, in the course of Descent, there arises an impulse or a desire to harm another, there is no way that this is your soul speaking to you. It is surely a corrupted or twisted element of your ego.

To give a concrete example, let's come back to the topic of sexuality. As part of the process of awakening the Below, you want to be able to completely give over control of your sexuality to your body deva (or your body's intelligence, if you prefer that terminology), and allow it to show you how it wants to experience pleasure and intimacy. However, this under no circumstances gives you free license to engage in sexual activity that is harmful or hurtful to others. In other words, you need to figure out a way to totally surrender to the Below while also maintaining some firm lines that you refuse to cross no matter what. This may seem like an impossible paradoxical task, but it's a balancing act that you simply must do.

That being said, if you do experience impulses to harm others, you shouldn't bottle them up or push them away either. The surrendering process is about including, not denying. The proper response is to sit with the feeling and allow it to unpack itself, to express what it is trying to say, and thereby to untangle itself. But even as you welcome the potentially harmful impulses to move through you, you must have a strong resolve to never, ever act upon them. Experiencing passing feelings of rage, greed, lust, or of wanting to lash out at or control others is a normal part of the Descent because these impulses are normal parts of everyone's unconscious. However, if you ever feel that such thoughts are becoming compulsive, or you question your ability to resist acting on them, that is a red flag indicating that you need to talk with a therapist or spiritual counselor.

Uncontrollable compulsions to harm yourself or others are in many cultural traditions around the globe considered to be examples of possession by an evil spirit. This brings us to another kind of boundary that you need to have firmly in place. Entering into the Below, you will certainly encounter many energies and entities that seem autonomous and external to you. As we have discussed, nearly all of them will eventually turn out to be parts of your own being. They only seem external to you because you have repressed or denied them. In the end, they are revealed to be previously unconscious parts of you that, once fully awakened, become integral parts of your majestic wholeness.

However, it is possible that during your time in the Below you may encounter energies or entities that you truly believe are not part of you. For example, you might run into a ghost, spirit, or other entity or energy that you feel does not have a positive intent toward you. One of the lessons you need to learn in order to navigate the Below safely is how to clear such negative entities/energies out of your space. There are many ways of doing this using ritual, incantations, prayers, invocations, visualizations, and other techniques. You can find many specific techniques if you look into the books in the further readings section.

In my view, however, it's critical to balance setting boundaries or banishing rituals with a compassionate concern for the well-being of all. Wishing for the utter destruction of any being is an unhealthy and unenlightened form of violence. Also, it's important to keep this door open because, in the end, you'll probably come to recognize that this unwelcome presence is actually just another aspect of your unconscious you have yet to accept. Therefore, look for techniques like "compassionate depossession" and others that focus on helping malevolent spirits to transform rather than on destroying them.

Another type of boundary that is critical to uphold is what I call your "energetic bubble." The idea here is to minimize collateral damage when working out your traumas and complexes in the Below. You must recognize that your feelings, reactions, and egoic dramas that arise in the course of doing this work are all projections of your own mind, and you must work hard to not involve other people in them. If you find yourself working out some past trauma or situation that involved another person, you do not need to contact that person and drag them into your process. If you find yourself feeling regret for past actions, you do not need to reopen someone else's wounds in order to heal yours.

The same goes for positive feelings or even blessings. To give you a quick example, just a few weeks ago, my wife was approached at work by a total stranger who claimed she had a dream about her. The woman was emphatic that in her dream she had received a message from God and she simply had to share it with my wife, and she was quite insistent that my wife had to allow her to do a blessing for her. She made these pronouncements right in the middle of an office where my wife was surrounded by coworkers and was trying to do her job. The woman would not go away, waited until my wife was on break, and then accosted her with the insistence that they meet privately somewhere so that she could perform some kind of ceremony.

In this encounter with my wife, the woman clearly breached her energetic bubble by pushing her spiritual agenda in a way that encroached on my wife's freedom and comfort. Now, she may just have been delusional, but for argument's sake, let's say that she had an authentic imaginal experience in which she legitimately had perceived herself to have received an important message from God. Even so, surely there would be a better way to share this. Could she have written my wife a quick note and left her phone number inviting her to speak about it if she felt so moved? Could she have delivered the blessing silently and unobtrusively from across the room, without involving my wife at all? My intention here isn't to dictate how the encounter should have gone; my point is to encourage you to reflect on how to maintain your own energetic integrity without heaping it onto others who might find your overtures unwelcome or uncomfortable.

I will mention one last boundary that's important as you navigate the Below. As we've said many times, the Descent can be terrifying and dangerous. You therefore need to exert your spiritual sovereignty and discernment when it comes to determining how much is too much at any given moment. Here's Misha talking about her experience exploring her limits:

> In my case, it's taken a lot of healing with skillful guidance for me to develop the capacities that make surrendering likely to result in becoming less, rather than more, broken. If trauma activation is too intense, it can result in exacerbation and retraumatization rather than healing. At the same time, part of the healing process has been about realizing that I can go through flashbacks and other kinds of dysregulated experiences, and successfully come out of them. Part of the learning for me has been that these experiences can feel like "it will be like this always," but I've learned that this is not objective reality/truth.
>
> Since my most recent retreat, part of the shifting has been around allowing myself to experience trauma reactivation. It's been difficult to let go of the resistance to the experiences that generate unpleasantness. Many times in my past I've been hijacked by PTSD activations, yet recently there have been times I've been able to surrender and let the dreaded experience happen. One time, after feeling pierced through as if by multiple small projectiles, what showed up was vulnerability and a lovely, pure innocence.
>
> As time went on, however, I ended up in a PTSD flare-up, and for a couple of weeks I was floundering. I had to significantly shift how I was practicing. I had to stop diving in to any activation that was happening and instead intensively practice mindful witnessing, noticing sensations, staying out of the mind and thoughts, and doing lots of grounding. At first this was on and off for most of the hours of the day, particularly at night. Over a three-week period, the activations gradually reduced to a much more manageable level.
>
> Interestingly, allowing what was showing up—even resistance—to be present was key during all the parts of the retreat and post-retreat experiences. It's the type of skillful engagement that changed.

CHAPTER FIVE

Spiritual emergency or Descent into the Below?

Over the past few decades, the phrase "spiritual emergency" has become widespread among many spiritual communities in the West. Inspired by the transpersonal psychologists Christina and Stan Groff, the term typically refers to a crisis of a spiritual nature, or one brought on by spiritual practice, presenting a severe mental or physical challenge to the experiencer. But exactly what constitutes a spiritual emergency versus the expected or normal kinds of challenges associated with the awakening process has always remained an open question.

Recent studies have shown that whether or not spiritual phenomena are experienced as emergencies is in large part due to the experiencer's ability to interpret their experiences in positive ways. Extreme spiritual phenomena that happen without adequate context tend to provoke terror, confusion, and dysregulation. However, when one is able to make sense of these phenomena and fit them into a larger framework that is meaningful, they can come to be accepted as challenging—though not necessarily destabilizing—parts of the awakening process.

One of the main purposes of this book has been to identify some of the weirder, darker, more unusual kinds of phenomena that can arise in the course of a spiritual awakening, and to provide a helpful reframing of these. The hypothetical reader I have in mind, the one who I surmise will be most interested in what I have to say in these pages, is someone who has had at least a substantial taste of the Above (i.e., awakening to nonduality, emptiness, universal love, or divinity), but then has unexpectedly found themselves in the midst of a Descent. How this descent happened will be unique from person to person, but I am imagining that such a reader is at present thoroughly confused as to why their experience doesn't match the Above-based descriptions of awakening shared in their spiritual traditions or communities. Perhaps certain aspects of the Below are completely unknown within their circles, or perhaps they are actively demonized. I imagine that they are frightened, and perhaps are even experiencing this all as an existential threat.

What I have attempted to provide here in these pages is a framework for such a reader to reinterpret their experiences by placing them into a healthy, meaningful narrative that will both provide comfort and deepen their awakening process. Once someone has accepted the Below as a normal part of spirituality, one can transition from framing the Descent as a spiritual emergency to appreciating it as a great, mysterious gift.

In this chapter, I will attempt to show this kind of reframing in action through some case studies. Each one takes a series of events that were at the time interpreted as some kind of crisis, and demonstrates how they might be reinterpreted in light of the materials and models presented in this book.

When to get help

Before we get into the case studies that represent the heart of this chapter, let's take a moment to acknowledge the limitations of our approach. It's simply not the case that reframing one's experiences can solve every problem all of the time. The Below sometimes does have real, innate dangers.

In the first place, because of how closely the body is linked with the unconscious mind (Jung held that the body is actually *part* of the unconscious), the psychic turmoil you experience while awakening the Below almost always manifests physically. It is therefore highly likely that you will experience a range of uncomfortable bodily sensations, symptoms, or actual illnesses as you go through the alchemical and energetic transformations of the Descent and Return.

In my own case, these physical discomforts included insomnia, heart palpitations, and acid reflux. Other people I know have experienced chronic pain, migraines, temporary paralysis, and other weird ailments. To be safe, it is always advisable to consult a medical doctor to rule out any serious conditions when such things arise. There also may be particular value in being treated by a practitioner of energy medicine (acupuncture, Reiki, etc.).

Aside from the possibility of physical danger, it is a near certainty that you will experience mental and emotional upheaval. It may even be difficult to distinguish between the experience of the Below and serious mental health issues. Confusing overlaps between the two occur because certain types of psychosis can often have spiritual themes or content, and certain types of spiritual experiences can mimic the symptoms of mental illness. It's not for nothing that Joseph Campbell was once quoted as saying "the psychotic drowns in the same waters in which the mystic swims with delight."

Because certain mystical experiences share a lot of common ground with madness, there are some red flags that are prudent to keep in mind. First and foremost is the inability to distinguish spiritual experiences from the everyday world. Believing in strange things is not a mental illness. Nor is seeing deities, spirits, ghosts, fairies, aliens, or other visions in your mind's eye, in dreams, during spiritual practice, in a twilit room when you first wake up from sleep, or in other liminal spaces. On the other hand, if you are seeing these in your visual field, in broad daylight, mixed in with your eyesight in a way that you can't tell the difference between the ordinary world and the imaginal world, those are hallucinations, and you should get checked out by a mental health professional.

Likewise, if you've become confused about what's happening within your own psyche versus consensus reality, or if spiritual phenomena are completely incapacitating you, or if you find yourself uncontrollably talking about imaginal events in inappropriate social settings, or if you become suicidal, or if you have strong or persistent thoughts or impulses to harm other people, these are all also clear signs that you need to seek help right away.

It also may just be that one day you realize you can't handle the intensity of the phenomena you are experiencing without some support. If that happens, don't hesitate to reach out for help. While it may feel like you are alone, there are many knowledgeable guides and counselors who can help you to navigate this territory. I've listed below some organizations I like to point people to, who specialize in supporting people who find themselves in an acute spiritual emergency:

- American Center for the Integration of Spiritually Transformative Experiences (aciste.org)
- Cheetah House (cheetahhouse.org)
- Spiritual Emergence Network (www.spiritualemergence.org)
- Spiritual Crisis Network (spiritualcrisisnetwork.uk)
- Spiritual Emergence Anonymous (spiritualemergenceanonymous.org)

Case study 1: Oholomo's descending Kundalini

So far in this book, I have tended to suggest that the Descent is a gradual step-by-step process of sinking into the Below, with a slow and steady peeling back of its layers. However, for some people, the Descent into the Below can happen quite precipitously. For me, it happened extremely rapidly as a result of a certain type of Kundalini opening.

Kundalini is a generic term that is used in contemporary Western spiritual communities for many kinds of energetic phenomena that arise in the course of spiritual practice. The most common form of Kundalini is primarily a pranic or energetic opening. This kind of Kundalini generally feels like the body comes alive with tingling, electric, bioenergetic, or subtle vibrations. Typically, these sensations begin at the base of the spine and move in an upwards trajectory up the midline of the body to culminate in the head. This kind of Kundalini is normally associated with Above-oriented spirituality. The ideal is that this moving energy opens up the entire chakra system, culminating in the opening of the spiritual centers in the third eye and crown, which lead to mystical experiences of the Above.

In East Asian traditions, there is a similar notion of the awakening of the body's qi. Here, the sensations trace a pattern up the backside of the body and down the front in a continuous loop, leading to both spiritual development and physical vitality—in other words, energetically connecting the Above and the Middle.

Both of these kinds of energetic openings are highly valued and much spoken about. However, there's another type of Kundalini opening that is more rarely mentioned, which is the kind that is more associated with the Below. This also can involve flows of prana, but the primary characteristic is that it feels like the body-mind is fundamentally torn open. The energy system goes completely haywire, the body goes into shock, the unconscious portion of the psyche is suddenly ripped from its slumber and spills out into awareness. This kind of Kundalini feels like something utterly other has taken over the body and mind, something that is at once both completely alien and also unspeakably magnificent. It simultaneously feels sublimely divine and ferociously dark, total ecstasy and also sheer terror.

The result of an opening like this is often that the journeyer is flung down through the Below at lightning speed. There is an explosion of imaginal phenomena of all kinds, spirits, energies, bodily autonomy, sexuality, ancestral and past life materials, nature spirits and elementals, and likely even the Abyss in very short order. What normally might take years of slow discovery somehow all bursts forth in a few weeks or even days.

As I have already intimated, my own Descent was sparked by just such a Kundalini event during which I experienced the serpentine goddess I now call Bachué taking over my body. When I say it was a "descending" Kundalini, the downward direction was, for me, a visceral experience. As I was on a meditation walk in my neighborhood, I felt a surge of blissful energy shoot up my back and out the top of my head into the sky. But soon enough, an intense torrent rushed back down through the core of my body. The sensation was like a firehose had been inserted into my mouth. It was so strong that I staggered and nearly was knocked to my knees as I gagged and dry-heaved into my neighbor's bushes. The accompanying imaginal vision was of a massive black snake rushing down my gullet, and depositing some kind of milk-like liquid into my dantian. From that point onwards, I felt like there was a glimmering, buzzing portal to the Below located in my abdomen. (First, I experienced this as a vibrant black gemstone, later as a dark tunnel down through my perineum into the Abyss.)

Other people I have spoken to describe other kinds of downward-directed sensations. Something that seems to be quite common is strong sensations in the soles of the feet. (In my case, they felt hot for a few months, like I was walking on coals.) However, the main reason I am calling this descending Kundalini is not because of the directionality of the energy flows, but rather to specify a Kundalini event that bursts open the Below. In my case, having spent a year in the Above in a blissful state of nondual perception and thinking I was enlightened, I was suddenly hurled into the Descent. In the space of about two weeks, I had energetic upheaval, visionary experiences, and spirit visitations of all kinds.

Here's how I described the Kundalini event and its aftermath in the journal I was keeping at the time, the full text of which I have made public on my website, AwakeningTheBelow.com. The following is excerpted, condensed, and slightly edited as usual:

> I'm walking outdoors when I have a vision that all the trees around me suddenly transform into multi-headed snakes spurting up out of the ground. I feel my whole body begin vibrate, and a current of tingling sensations emerges from deep inside my pelvis and flows up my spine. When it reaches the top of my head, snakes spray out my skull, a canopy of cobra heads looming above me. I feel energized and immensely strong.
>
> The feeling expands until my whole body is filled with squirming snakes. They spiral around my limbs, my torso, and my spine, squeezing me tenderly in their coils while gliding across my skin. Their slick, liquid slithering is intensely pleasurable. As they glide beneath my skin, the ecstasy becomes unbearable. I can't contain the energy. I involuntarily start making grimacing faces, and hissing sounds come out of my mouth.
>
> The feelings of pleasure intensify even further, building and building until my body explodes in waves after waves of shuddering full-body orgasms wrapping around themselves. The snakes and I penetrate each other sexually—in, out, and through every orifice, in every conceivable way.
>
> Then, a black serpentine demon-like goddess fills my body. Her lower body rises out of a dark ocean of serpents. Her scaly legs coil and intertwine. At her waist, a shift from the reptilian to the feminine. A youthful body with voluptuous breasts and skin black as midnight. Her face is the sun. Her arms are raised overhead. She's holding a golden orb, with rays of blinding light extending in all directions. She is the full spectrum from terrifying darkness to angelic radiance, connecting underworld with the heavens.
>
> We are not one but not two. I am the Snake Mother's son and also her lover, and she is also my body itself. There's something

about her breasts and nipples. I have an instinctual urge to suck on them. Yes, there's an obvious feeling of sexual arousal behind this impulse, but also something much, much deeper. A distant muscle memory that is only dimly coming back into consciousness, connecting suckling a breast with warmth, safety, and satiety. With life itself.

I suck, and the breastmilk begins to flow. Warm, nourishing, white ambrosia. But then: a gush, a geyser, an ocean of milk going down my throat. A rushing stream too powerful to contain. Mother, I am drowning.

Her black breast transforms into a gigantic serpent that suddenly descends from the sky and enters my mouth, filling my throat, my stomach, my intestines in a downwards torrent. The snake disgorges a load of the Goddess's breastmilk deep in my belly. It is overwhelming, and I find myself in a stupor, gagging and retching.

The white milk coalesces to form a fist-sized black diamond in the center of my pelvis. Her seed has been planted. I have been impregnated with her mysterious essence. Some kind of treasure will eventually be born.

Is this a gateway to enlightenment or a portal to insanity? I am filled with panic. She is telling me that I am safe, but all I can do is tremble in fear and beg her for mercy. Ecstasy gives way to a deep well of terror.

For days I hardly have slept at all. I am anxious. No appetite. I feel like I have come down with the flu. I feel exhausted and lack the ability to focus on anything. I question my sanity, my health, and my strength to walk this path. But I do not have a choice. The only way forward is straight into the serpent's gaping mouth. This is not an invitation; it is a mandate. There is no turning back now.

The intense Kundalini opening seems to have unleashed a ton of fluttering, stinging, and itching across the sternum as well as heart palpitations. My chest feels quite locked up at the moment. I checked with a cardiologist and everything is normal, so I assume that this is all just the growing pains of the energies opening. I am now sitting with the unpleasant sensations and allowing them to pass through.

With the initial awakening, it sometimes felt like I was taller than usual. Like I was seeing things from a location a few inches above the top of my head. These days, it sometimes feels like I'm half as tall as I am. Like I'm looking out at the world through eyes located in my abdomen.

Other strange energetic phenomena have been taking place as well. I feel like my sense of smell is supercharged. I can smell a flower or a person 100 feet away. Is this a siddhi of superhuman smell? I've frequently felt like I am not in a body at all, just suspended in empty space. A couple of times when I had this perception, it felt like some other entity might be trying to enter my body. A pang of fear, and I have to stomp my feet around while walking briskly in order to force myself to return back into my body. I'm awake for an hour or two in the middle of the night, every night. A constant burning feeling like fire in my lower abdomen. And, I've also developed a serious case of chronic acid reflux.

As I was entirely unprepared for this kind of cataclysmic event, I was completely confounded when it happened. I think it's inevitable that any journeyer who is suddenly ejected from the peaceful serenity of the Above and thrown into this kind of turmoil would find themselves radically destabilized. Someone who didn't have any context and wasn't familiar with any of the phenomena we've been examining in this book could understandably assume that they have gone mad—a psychotic break or sudden onset of schizophrenia, perhaps. That certainly was the case for me, and it took many months for me to eventually come to terms with what had happened.

Of course everyone's experience is unique, but I've provided my story here to give you a general idea of some of the phenomena that might occur in a downward Kundalini, precisely so that you don't panic and assume something is wrong with you. If you are having a descending Kundalini, I know from personal experience it's a lot to cope with. You will likely feel like you're right at the limit of what you can handle, on the razor's edge of madness.

Being afraid and confused like this is unavoidable. But, if you can somehow manage to surrender to the process, you will eventually gain confidence that you can actually handle it. You can gradually relax into the Descent and start to receive its blessings. Believe it or not, in the end, you will find this hair-raising roller-coaster journey to have been a tremendous gift. One day, you will be grateful for, and remember fondly, every step of this process—even this one.

Case study 2: Misha's identity fractures apart

In this account of crisis, Misha, who we heard from numerous times in the preceding pages, shared with me the following account of the fracturing of her personality into "parts." Let's let her tell her story first, and then we can reinterpret and reframe it along the lines we've been exploring in this book:

> About nine years ago, I was intensively plumbing the depths of the meaning, function, and value of the Twelve Steps, as well as using a homegrown framework for exploring the issues of life, death, and my relationship with those. In addition to engaging in regular meditation, breathwork, and prayer, I was doing a lot of inquiry and contemplation. Increasingly, I withdrew from reality and was experiencing life through the filter of past trauma. I began referring to myself as a collective organism with adult selves, plus child and teenaged parts.
>
> During this time, I frequently regressed into a childlike state. At times I could vividly see in my mind's eye, and energetically feel, how my bedroom window opened onto a castle and a magical land in the yard beyond. It felt to me like this fantasy land was overlaid on the physical world. In its own way it was as real as the ordinary world, and I was the Princess. Other times I would connect with the spirit of Eagle and let Eagle dance with and through me, "flying" around the house.
>
> When I showed up at anonymous support group telephone meetings, increasingly I was speaking in a child's tone of voice. I began using a child's nickname, and started insisting that name be used. I'd feel irritated if I showed up in that child state and people called me by the adult name by which they had known me.
>
> In the deepest part of the crisis, when I got triggered, it would take as long as a day and a half to calm down enough to get myself to bed. Due to extreme levels of anxiety, I slept with the room lights on and the bedroom door locked. I slept fully clothed, including shoes, with a kitchen knife under my pillow. My bed was a "scary zone." I'd visualize Dog curled up under my bed to alert me in case of approaching danger, and Bear curled up behind me for protection and comfort.
>
> Eventually, a person in the group whom I trusted suggested I talk with a counselor. They persisted with increasing insistence until

I acted on the suggestion. By then, I was significantly homebound, disabled, and incapacitated, so trying to get to in-person appointments on a regular basis was impossible. My once a month grocery runs took the rest of the month to recover from, and I spent most of my time in bed on high doses of prescription pain medication. Eventually, I discovered that a counselor I'd worked with decades before was still in practice on the other side of the continent. I reached out by phone and left a message, hoping to connect.

Soon, I received a message in a gentle voice from my old counselor, saying we could "pick up the stitch." I felt relieved I'd be getting help from this trusted person. Because I lived so far away, I was the first client he began working with over a video platform (this was more than four years before the COVID-19 outbreak). Over several calls, he gradually and gently drew me in, soliciting information about my state along the way.

I don't recall spiritual emergence being addressed overtly in counseling. So I wasn't getting any direct spiritual guidance around that part of the crisis. Instead, our weekly sessions seemed to be focused around trauma recovery. However, my counselor was spiritually awakened (though I didn't recognize that at the time) and was part of the Spiritual Emergence Network. In addition, he had a great deal of clinical expertise working with adult women survivors of chronic, developmental childhood sexual abuse. So I was in good hands in both those regards.

Practices that kept me highly focused on being in the present moment and out of dissociative states helped a lot. Also practices that helped soothe my jangled nervous system and helped me feel safe. Executing mandala art of the symbolic images that appeared in my visions was part of the therapeutic process. Sometimes I'd spend twenty to forty hours on a given image, which kept me grounded in the ordinary world while still in touch with the imaginal.

Besides psychotherapy, I continued participating in Twelve Step programs during this time. I also received lots of help and support from my closest friends. I found comfort in spiritual books and recordings that resonated with me. Tara Brach was particularly soothing. Things finally began calming down a lot, and the next round of major awakening shifts began about two and a half years after this one.

Going through the above account in detail, we can recognize a lot of the hallmarks of the Descent. The practices that Misha was working with at the time of the onset of the crisis seem to have provoked the collapse of her centralized, unified sense of self. That, of course, is one of the principal purposes of inquiry and meditation. But, instead of experiencing this collapse of the self as a blissful emptiness or a divine oneness as one typically does in an Above-based awakening, for whatever reason, Misha's system was wired in such a way that she was thrust into the Below.

In the absence of a unifying self to provide coherence for her identity, Misha began experiencing various previously unconscious aspects of her being as autonomous entities ("parts," in her language). She doesn't explicitly mention this in the narrative above, but no doubt some of those childlike parts had important messages that needed to be expressed regarding childhood memories, traumas, and wounds (at one point, she mentions having been abused while young). Those repressed parts demanded to be recognized and accepted, for example, by insisting on being called by their proper names.

At the same time that was happening, Misha's imaginal world also began to open up with visions of a fantasy landscape with herself as a princess. She also experienced some kind of light trance state or semi-possession by the eagle spirit.

Like most people going through the Descent, Misha's system was overwhelmed by the experience and she became energetically dysregulated. She fell into a morass of anxiety, with increased fatigue and pain. She also suffered from insomnia, which is one of the most common energetic side effects of awakening. In the depths of the night, she was accompanied both by fearsome dark energies as well as by imaginal animal companions who protected her.

All of these phenomena we have considered in detail in previous chapters. But it sounds like Misha didn't have any context for what she was experiencing at the time. Her therapist wasn't familiar with the Below, and she had no specific practices in her repertoire that would encourage her to dive head-on into the underworld aspects that were emerging.

Nevertheless, on balance it sounds like working with the therapist on the underlying trauma was enormously helpful for her. (I do think that everyone who finds themselves confronting childhood abuse could benefit from connecting with an experienced counselor.) In addition, she mentions finding artistic expression of her imaginal visions to be beneficial. Also, grounding practices that helped keep her out of dissociative states and soothed the nervous system. Of course, the specific things that worked for her wouldn't necessarily work for everyone, but the general notions of support, engagement, and grounding are, in my opinion, universally advisable.

Fortunately for Misha, with the help of her trusted counselor, she was able to navigate her opening to the Below successfully, and it opened doors for her growth along her spiritual path. She now provides guidance and support for others going through spiritual emergency under the name Alleia Arising. Others are not always so lucky, as we'll see in the next case study.

Case study 3: After the meditation retreat

This narrative was publicly posted by a user called HouseOnFire on DharmaOverground.org, a forum dedicated to meditation phenomena, on October 29, 2020. I've made a few edits, just to clean up spelling, fix typos, and add some punctuation for clarity. I also omitted parts of the post at the beginning and end where the author is referencing other materials in the forum.

> When I showed up at the Goenka retreat last January I was very much there to try to save myself from the mess I was making of my life. The first few days of Goenka are just observing the sensations of the breath at and below the nostrils. I had been drinking, smoking weed, and drinking a lot of coffee, so these days were a detox for me and I slept whenever I wasn't meditating.
>
> Then on day four we were taught the Goenka body scan method and things changed. I picked up each new element of the body scan instruction quite easily and I attribute this to the months of concentration meditation I'd been doing.... I quickly became aware of subtle vibrations all through my body and could "play" with them at will.
>
> The rest of the course was extremely trippy. Each night I slept less but awoke with full energy, immediately aware of the subtle energies. In my non-meditative time I started playing a game I called "what drug does it feel like I'm on." Sometimes it was acid, sometimes MDMA or mushrooms.

In Goenka language, "I passed many sankaras." During mediation I would find a dark or painful area in the awareness of my body, hang out with it, and watch it dissolve. Moments or hours later I'd feel some intense emotion, usually sadness, and then cry for a while. Then later still I'd have a memory come up—the time my parents installed a lock on the outside of my bedroom door and how I'd screamed and kicked the door down when they tried to use it, or whatever.

Where in my drinking and depression I'd felt mentally dull, now I seemed to be able to think in complete paragraphs, and at one point I decided to try to make sense of my life. This is where I got into trouble by remembering every important thing that ever happened to me. I had a single thought process go on for six hours uninterrupted until the thoughts started to go in slow motion and I found I couldn't verbally cognate anymore. I could speak and knew what I was doing, but I couldn't say words in my head. It was very strange.

So the course ends, I get to finally meet the other meditators, and then go home. It was a long drive home and I didn't get there until about 3 a.m. Having woken up about this time the day before, I've now been awake for twenty-four hours. As I look at myself in the mirror before bed, I notice that my eyes and facial expression look a lot like pictures I've seen of Ram Dass where he looks totally blasted on bliss. Also—strangely, as I am a dude and don't normally think about myself this way—I think that I look incredibly beautiful and lean in and give my mirror-self a little kiss. Finally in bed, I make a little bath of love for myself out of subtle vibrations and lay back saying "anything, anything." It is the most contented moment of my adult life.

This is when shit gets weird. Suddenly my body starts rolling around on the bed all on its own. I kinda feel like I'm being pushed around but I can tell the energy is coming from the inside. I get the sense that I could stop it if I really wanted to, but it definitely doesn't feel volitional. As I've just completed a ten-day course where the main focus was letting things rise up as they will without reacting, I decide to go with it.

Pretty soon I'm up off the bed and dancing. "Okay," I think, "I've got the dancing mania, cool." Then I'm spinning my arms all around and my finger brushes across my chest and in a way that feels ... seductive. The sensation at this point is hard to describe but I can only say that I became a sexy woman. I felt that I was a woman and I felt sexy as fuck. I strutted around the room feeling just so hot.

Then I felt strong hands push me onto the bed and begin to ravish me sexually. I went through all the positions of sex as a woman and felt all the emotion if not all the sensation. But I'm talking raucous sex and I moaned and screamed as would be appropriate. When this ended maybe twenty minutes later, I decided I'd better go tell my roommate what was going on as she'd obviously heard me. As I talked to her I kept feeling hands trying to pull me back into the bedroom and I could feel my gender changing from male to female and back again. When I allowed the female version to take over I moved and spoke in a feminine way and was super affectionate towards my roommate.

The problem was it didn't stop. All night long, I had these bizarre sexual experiences with my ghost lover even though I was exhausted. By the time morning came I was panicking a little. What the hell was going on? Was I a trans woman and this was my subconscious way of letting me know? Was I possessed by a fucking spirit? Was all of this shit random?

I called a friend and he gave me the shitty advice to go see a medium. I did so and thank god she just said that I should call the meditation teacher. His explanation was that my subconscious mind had become too intertwined with my conscious mind and that sleep would fix me. But that night sleep was again impossible, and on the third day I had my friends take me to the hospital.

I'll spare you the story of the hospital other than to tell you that when they gave me Ativan and Seroquel it felt like I was being blasted through a DMT tunnel and I only slept for an hour or so. A week later, I was discharged with a prescription for a powerful antipsychotic in hand. After a month or so I could sleep without the drugs but I became severely depressed. It's only in the last few weeks I've felt like I've come out of the depression and started meditating again …

Did my experience mean something? What the hell was that?

This account really moves me because of the obvious confusion the journeyer underwent. It also is a clear example to me of the potentially dire consequences of misunderstanding the Below. As before, let's go through it bit by bit, comparing the experiences described by HouseOnFire against those detailed in this book.

In the first place, let's note the context in which these events occurred. The meditation retreat described here (which the poster simply calls "Goenka") is a common Above-oriented variety of Theravada Buddhist vipassana meditation. In these courses, participants are encouraged to focus entirely on Above-based perspectives and there is no teaching related to, or even mention of, the Below. We can also notice that HouseOnFire went to this retreat with the idea of escaping or fixing "the mess" of his life—that is to say, he was seeking to transcend rather than embody his humanity.

As HouseOnFire began to participate in the retreat, he noticed the psychedelic effects of high-dosage meditation starting to kick in. As the defenses of his ego-wall started to become more porous, he began to experience various repressed emotions and traumas arising to be seen and witnessed.

What happens next is evident of a severe lack of grounding. HouseOnFire participates with full intensity in the retreat (which, by the way, I happen to know requires ten or more hours of seated meditation per day with yoga, qigong, or other grounding practices explicitly prohibited). Then, he makes a long drive and deprives himself of sleep even further. Because of the sensitivity of his condition (whether due to the retreat or other factors it is impossible to say), he rapidly plunges further and further into the Below.

The homoerotic moment in front of the mirror, the gender changes, the spontaneous sexual energies, the feeling that this was happening because of an autonomous external entity such as a ghost or spirit, and the loss of control or feeling of being possessed are all things we've discussed in detail throughout this book. HouseOnFire reaches out to a friend, a medium, and the meditation teacher, but no one seems to be able to help him make sense of his experience. Like many others who perceive themselves to be in a spiritual emergency, HouseOnFire winds up in the hospital, where doctors treat him for psychosis. He seems to have eventually stabilized with medication, but has lingering depression as well as lack of meaning or context for the experiences he has gone through.

Could HouseOnFire's experiences have gone differently? Maybe, maybe not. Perhaps he has a propensity toward manic or psychotic symptoms that would eventually have been triggered by any kind of spiritual practice. Perhaps his best resort in that moment really was hospitalization and pharmaceutical interventions. But, what if instead of a complete lack of context and support, he had read this very book and was able to reframe his experiences in a positive and supportive way? What if he had known how to ground himself and engage with the Below, rather than getting sucked away into extreme dysregulation and disorientation? We can only speculate, but I would wager that his engagement with the Below would very likely have been much more manageable and meaningful than it was.

Case study 4: Jack's dark night of the soul

One last case study I'd like to introduce is that of my friend Jack. We've heard a lot from Jack in the preceding pages, in particular about his experiences of the dark imaginal and his close relationship with deities, ancestors, and other spirits. But these relationships deepened and developed over the course of many years, and, at least at first, his process of Descent was anything but smooth.

The following account is excerpted (also edited and some pieces moved around a bit) from a YouTube talk titled "Heartfelt Support as You Move through the Dark Night" he recorded for his My Rising Rose channel in 2024. Here is Jack's story about his own Dark Night, including his thoughts on the ultimate meaning of these kinds of experiences:

> I went through a quite sudden spiritual transformation that happened when I was twenty-six—that's eleven years ago. It started out very spontaneous and easy. It felt like everything was flowing very well, and it felt really clear and open and peaceful. I would go in and out of states of presence and experience deep peace of mind. And I was so uplifted because I'd finally found something that was breaking me free from all of the pain that I'd been suffering through for most of my life before that point.
>
> This continued on for about a year, I would say, until I had a Kundalini awakening that was similar to a near-death experience. After that Kundalini awakening, my consciousness was radically changed. It was like the volume had just been turned up, or a dimmer switch had just been turned up. I began to see and feel energy, and I had out of body experiences where I was meeting all these different beings, angels, and deities and having telepathic communication with them.

That was obviously amazing on one level, and on another it was pretty intense and it sent my nervous system into shock. For quite a while after that Kundalini awakening, I was very ungrounded. In the first week afterwards, my sense of myself was so shaken that I was not coherently inside of my body. That was confusing and disorienting, and I didn't really have anyone to talk to about it. I had quite a long period out of work, about six months off for sick leave. Just walking out of the house felt incredibly difficult. Just the basics of going to the shop and getting food felt like it was the hardest thing in the world because my energy field was so confused. It was overwhelming to try to do anything.

I went back to live with my mom in the countryside in England. I thought I would be there for maybe a month or two, but what happened was that I really went into the Dark Night of the Soul, and I ended up being there for two and a half years. And what I found was that the more time that I was at my mom's, the deeper I was descending into some kind of really dark and challenging place. I was meeting all these different parts of myself that I had been running from.

My childhood was really traumatizing. Even the way that I entered this world was traumatizing. I nearly died when I was born, and if you know much about the way that trauma is held inside of the body, then you'll know that a traumatic birth that is left unaddressed can predispose one to lots of anxieties and suffering later in life. Especially if they're in a family that is abusive physically and emotionally, and neglectful, which mine was. And then, when I was in my teenage years, I was using alcohol and drugs to cope with that, to push all that down. But now I had stopped drinking and stopped taking drugs, and had gone through this spiritual transformation where my awareness had become much brighter. And what was happening was that my bright awareness that wasn't being suppressed through drugs and alcohol anymore was now casting a light on everything that was inside my body and my mind: all of those things that I was afraid of, and all the things that I'd been running from for so long.

All of that had a really profound effect on my body. I was absolutely exhausted all the time and could barely get out of bed. But I couldn't really sleep either. I would have intense nightmares pretty much every night. For a full year, I'd wake up around 3 a.m.

and would just be sweating from the nightmares that I was having. I would only get a few hours' sleep at night, and then I'd be exhausted during the day.

Also, I was feeling real despair and feeling like I'm a loser because I'm in my late twenties and am living with my mom. Seeing other people and comparing myself to the way they're living their life, I was an absolute failure. I was studying medicine when I was eighteen. I was going to be a doctor, and I was going to be looked up to by the people around me. By this point in my life, I expected to be married with kids, having my own home and living really well by all social standards. And I had failed. I'm at my mom's house, I'm single, I'm in intense emotional pain every day, I'm unemployed. The people around me didn't understand what I was going through, either. Even family members treated me like I was just nothing.

At the same time, I was having these new openings in my mind where I could communicate with these deities who were telling me that everything was going the way it was meant to be going. They gave me this analogy. They showed me a vision in my mind of this old office building from the 1970s, and they were like, "Look, the carpet's outdated. The computer is really old and barely works. This office isn't fit for the modern world. It's not fit for purpose; it doesn't function well. We need to upgrade it." And, of course, the office here in this analogy was me: my mind, my state of consciousness, and all of the outdated things were all those old patterns that were running through me.

And what they were saying was, "Okay, we're going to update this office. We're going to get workers to come in with jackhammers, and they're going to tear up the floors, and we're going to redo it all. We're going to rip the walls down because they're all moldy. We're going to build new ones, we're going to get you new computers, and everything's going to be running fantastically. It's all going to be running great in a few years, but not now. And the funny thing is, you're not allowed to leave the office. You have to stay here, which means that you are going to have to endure the disruption of all the noise that we're making. But just know that this isn't going to last forever. There is going to be a time when this all ends, and you will be where you want to be."

Did you know that when a caterpillar goes into a chrysalis, it doesn't just transform into a butterfly? The caterpillar actually dissolves. It becomes a liquid, and it's from that liquid that the butterfly is formed. So if you're going through this kind of Dark Night right now, just know that this is what is happening to you. You're withdrawing into your chrysalis. And as you feel into that and explore it for yourself, you may find you can relax and accept what's happening. To go with this process rather than resisting it.

Waking up can be a quite sudden thing that can feel like it's going to solve all our problems. And as it starts to deepen, usually what happens is we realize that it's not going to. We realize that we're going to need to get our hands dirty, that we're going to have to scrub the dishes ourselves. And that can take time, and it can be messy and painful.

For me, this spiritual life, this unification with our divinity and with the world and with life: it's not about escaping suffering. It's about learning how to suffer well. It's about realizing that suffering is our cross, the heavy weight that we carry that is also the vehicle for our spiritual evolution and our maturation as human beings. Suffering makes us wise and compassionate. It teaches us how to let go. It inspires us to greater depths of love and joy and peace. It's the reality check that keeps us grounded, and it's the calling that pulls our spirit down from the heavens to embrace the earth.

Jack's story has many of the signs of a Descent. It is clear that he too had some kind of descending Kundalini event: an energetic opening that cracked open his unconscious and led him into the Below. This opening resulted in his being able to communicate with deities, spirits, and other entities, but it also left him energetically destabilized and hypersensitive. As Jack describes it, the overwhelming Dark Night experience that ensued for several years involved the emergence of many "different parts" of himself that he "had been running from for so long." These included his birth trauma, childhood traumas, and many of the "old patterns" that he had been employing to cope with these old wounds. He also confronted feelings of failure and self-loathing, nightmares, and other difficulties as the unconscious parts of his psyche were dredged up into consciousness.

What's different about Jack's experiences than those of Misha or HouseOnFire is that he had some explicitly supportive messages from his spirit guides that helped him to accept what was happening. His guides explained to him that he may experience discomfort for a while, but that he ultimately had nothing to fear. This message allowed him to surrender to the process for as long as it took to complete the transformation (in his case, about two and half years).

In the story he tells, you can see how Jack is able to reframe his own difficult experiences in order to place them into a meaningful and healing narrative that highlights the importance of suffering in the spiritual life. (In the original video, he also invokes the image of Jesus weeping in the Garden of Gethsemane over the prospect of being tortured to death, a powerful imaginal symbol of the sanctity of suffering if there ever was one.) This reframing is both a product of the darkness Jack encountered in the depths of his Dark Night, and also a support that helped carry him through and out the other side. Now, as a spiritual teacher, he is able to share this understanding with others who are going through a similarly difficult awakening process. In other words, this reframing is one of the elixirs Jack brought back from the Below and is now sharing with his community. I have no doubt that this reframing will allow you to do the same.

CHAPTER SIX

Benediction

As the book closes and we say goodbye, let's take a moment to recap the core ideas. First, the principal point of this book is to establish that there is an alternative form of awakening that is different than what you may hear about in Buddhist, Advaita, and similar circles—one that is far darker and weirder than you may be expecting. Whether or not this type of awakening happens to you apparently lies completely beyond your ability to control or predict. If this happens to you, you will likely need specialized advice and support that will differ markedly from the teachings that are most predominant in mainstream spirituality. That being said, there is nothing wrong with the Below, and there is nothing wrong with you.

Second, I've repeated this many times, but I can't stress it enough: the critical thing for you to do is to surrender to the Descent. If you stop fighting against it, this journey will take you to the darkest, most terrifying places in the depths of your being. But there, you will undergo the most astonishing transformation and discover the most precious gifts. The more you fight against this process, the more difficult this dissolution and rebirth will be.

Third, remember that the whole point of the journey through the Below is for you to find, accept, and honor every last bit of the totality of the cosmos, welcoming it all into the unimaginably sacred wholeness that you are. That process cannot be selective: you must welcome not only all of your Above parts of lightness and love, but also all of the dark and terrifying parts that are forgotten and repressed. The wholeness must equally include everything you think of as "yourself" and all of the parts of the cosmos that you have denied within yourself.

Lastly, once you have liberated the whole universe in this way, you will not be perfect. You will not be an all-knowing, all-powerful Buddha who transcends the human condition and dwells in eternal bliss. But you will find that your soul's gifts, your elixirs, will be able to freely flow out into the world in just the way that you were always perfectly designed to deliver them. Eventually, with time, this whole array of light and dark parts will become so well integrated into your system that you will not even need to pay attention to them anymore. They will spontaneously, perfectly, and automatically arise as and when needed, without any conscious effort, thought, or even noticing necessary on your part.

To experience this freedom and ease is your birthright and your destiny. Nevertheless, in order to arrive at such a place, it is required that you must go through the difficult, torturous, and dangerous process of the Descent and Return. Like a caterpillar, you must be completely liquidated before you can take flight. Like Christ, you must be tortured to death before you can take your seat in Heaven. Like a phoenix, you must be annihilated, totally burned down to nothing, before you can rise again from the ashes.

If you knew how difficult this journey would be and how much you would need to sacrifice, you would never have willingly embarked upon it. However, the fact that you've read this far tells me that you likely have no choice over the matter. There's something whispering to your soul, pulling you inexorably toward the metamorphosis. You've already passed the point of no return, swept up in the undertow.

As you are drawn by these dark currents down into the Abyss, hold out your hand so that I can pass along a parting gift. It's this book, which contains a map of the territory you may pass through in the months and years to come. This is my own elixir, which I brought up from the depths of the Below precisely so it could be shared with travelers just like you.

May this elixir be good medicine for you, my dear friend! May this book be a lighthouse in the storm, a balm for your pain. May it never cause harm or suffering in any way to any being. And, may it carry all the blessings and invitations of the Below to whosoever is ready to hear the call and take the plunge. Goodbye for now, but we shall meet again upon your Return.

www.ingramcontent.com/pod-product-compliance
Ingram Content Group UK Ltd.
Pitfield, Milton Keynes, MK11 3LW, UK
UKHW020836051025
463618UK00002B/35